ON THE AIR

THE GOLDEN AGE
OF MANITOBA RADIO

ON THE AIR

GARRY MOIR

GREAT PLAINS
PUBLICATIONS

Great Plains Publications
233 Garfield Street
Winnipeg, MB R3G 2M1
www.greatplains.mb.ca

Great Plains Publications gratefully acknowledges the financial support provided for its publishing program by the Government
of Canada through the Canada Book Fund; the Canada Council for the Arts; the Province of Manitoba through the Book Publishing
Tax Credit and the Book Publisher Marketing Assistance Program; and the Manitoba Arts Council.

Design & Typography by Relish New Brand Experience
Printed in Canada by Friesens

Library and Archives Canada Cataloguing in Publication

Moir, Garry, 1949-, author
     On the air: the golden age of Manitoba radio / Garry Moir.

ISBN 978-1-927855-26-3 (pbk.)

     1. Radio broadcasting--Manitoba--History. I. Title.

HE8699.C2M58 2015   384.54097127   C2014-907249-X

TABLE OF CONTENTS

PROLOGUE

CHAPTER ONE   "The Father Cometh"   11

CHAPTER TWO   Radio In a Tuxedo   21

CHAPTER THREE   Dust Storms, Teepee Tales, and Radio Fit For a King   37

CHAPTER FOUR   Radio at War   55

CHAPTER FIVE   The Original Six   71

CHAPTER SIX   Torrents and Tragedy   89

CHAPTER SEVEN   Rural Roots   97

CHAPTER EIGHT   Farmin' and Learnin'   113

CHAPTER NINE   Fab Fifties   123

CHAPTER TEN   The Sporting Life   133

CHAPTER ELEVEN   The Men with the Music   145

CHAPTER TWELVE   Yakety Yak   165

EPILOGUE   181

ACKNOWLEDGMENTS   183

BIBLIOGRAPHY   185

INDEX   188

PROLOGUE

People don't listen to the radio as much as they used to. Hardly breaking news. Nor do they listen in the same way. Listening to the radio was once a shared experience, with families gathered in their living room to hear the latest drama or hockey match. Today, radio listening is an individual exercise, most often occurring in a motor vehicle in the midst of rush hour traffic. In an age of the Internet, smart phones, iPods, specialty television and social networking, it is perhaps remarkable that anyone is tuning in to radio at all. No medium has been written off more often.

Yet, despite a fragmented media world, Canadian radio continues to chug along. According to CRTC statistics in 2013, radio generates over a billion dollars in revenue annually, employs over 10,000 people and provides local audiences with information, programming and advertising, not always easily accessible through other mediums.

There is no single explanation as to why radio continues to survive. Obviously, it is extremely adaptable. The Internet and podcasts have provided new outlets through which people can listen. The radio station website offers a new source of revenue. Radio can be cheaply produced. The cost of radio advertising is but a fraction of most other mediums. Radio's greatest strength, however, has been the one constant throughout its history: it is the most intimate of all media. The emotional attachment between broadcaster and listener, while impossible to quantify, is real. We have all experienced it. Hearing a familiar voice after a long journey, a flood of memories when a certain song is played, a friendly companion on a lonely night or an interview so riveting that, even though you've reached your destination, you wait in your vehicle to hear how the story ends. It is the reason the medium remains special.

The staying power of local radio is also a testament to the people who built it. In its first 50 years, radio broadcasting was an exercise in experimentation from both a technical and programming perspective. Initially, having no model to guide them, local broadcasters broke new ground, with Manitoba leading the country in numerous areas. The first commercial radio licence ever issued went to a station in Winnipeg. The province had the first publicly owned broadcasting station. The first FM radio station in western Canada began in Winnipeg, as did the first French language station in the west. And the list goes on.

The growth and development of radio in Manitoba did not come easily, yet the influence has been lasting. Radio has had a profound impact, contributing to our economic, political, social and cultural lives.

The dollar value of products sold by radio is incalculable, as is the amount of money raised for charities. From 1939 to 1945, radio contributed tirelessly to the war effort.

The industry launched the careers of numerous local musicians and artists, some of whom would go on to great stardom. Radio has provided jobs, both directly and indirectly. It has helped save lives and kept people informed in times of crisis. What listeners hear on the air today is the evolution of programming, production, journalism and technological advances in a medium Winnipeggers in 1910 described as "weird, mysterious, and supernatural."

Over the decades, many local broadcasters, both on-air and behind the scenes, have contributed significantly to the development of radio. However, a simple online search often turns up little or nothing about them. Some were creative, innovative visionaries. The medium has also attracted its full share of rogues and rascals. Each in their own way contributed to the color and mystique of the broadcasting business. In many instances, the hours were long, the pay poor and job security non-existent. Yet, after sitting in living rooms, coffee shops and bars chatting with those who were part of radio's first 50 years, there is one prevailing theme: these early broadcasters were deeply committed to their craft, and proud to be part of it. They lived, loved, laughed, informed, entertained, took risks and made mistakes. In the process, they built an industry.

CAPITOL
RADIO
DEMONSTRATION

CHAPTER ONE

"The Father Cometh"

Lee De Forest liked to describe himself as the "father of radio." Then again, the inventor from Council Bluffs, Iowa, was not one to suffer from lack of ego. "All my years I never doubt for a moment my genius," he wrote in his journal at Yale University. Later, a number of fellow students voted him "most conceited" as well as "homeliest" in class.

In 1910, few people thought of De Forest as father of radio. There were, in fact, many "fathers" emerging in the early part of the new century. In 1901, the Italian inventor Marconi had demonstrated sound could travel long distances without wires. The letter "S" had been transmitted in Morse code from England and was picked up by a Marconi receiver on the coast of Newfoundland. Five years later, on Christmas Eve, Canadian Reginald Aubrey Fessenden transmitted the first radio program over the airwaves. He played "O Holy Night" on his violin and read a passage from the Bible. His broadcast was transmitted from Brant Rock, Massachusetts and was picked up by several ships in the Atlantic Ocean. De Forest's contribution came in the form of a radio tube which he patented in 1907.

The device amplified sound coming into a receiver and was a huge step forward in making radio a practical and marketable commodity.

Why Lee De Forest chose to visit Winnipeg in April of 1910 has never been established. Perhaps it was to get away from the many distractions he was facing back home in New York. His second marriage was falling apart. His first supposedly was never consummated. He was facing fraud charges in the United States because of shady business dealings. There were also accusations he had stolen ideas from the Canadian inventor Fessenden and claimed them as his own. "It was a period of my deepest gloom," he would later write in his autobiography, *The Father of Radio*.

Opposite: Early radio was showcased in local theatres.
FOOTE COLLECTION MANITOBA ARCHIVES

The Winnipeg Tribune.

THE WEATHER: FINE Fine and warmer.

WINNIPEG, CANADA, TUESDAY, APRIL 19, 1910

No. 77.

OF NAVAL OF DOMINION

it Will Consist of Five be Under Control of heries Minister.

AFRICAN HUNTER RESPECTS LIONS

Man Who Guided Col. Roosevelt in Africa Speaks of Big Game.

"Then it Happened"
Our Daily Discontinued Story.

CONSTABLE SAVES A MAN FROM DEATH

Patrolman Street Discovers House on Fire While Occupant is Sleeping.

BOSTON MARATHON WON BY CANADIAN

Al. Cameron, of New Amherst, Finishes Ahead of Big Field.

Private Members in the Manitoba House

ALBERT PREFONTAINE.

WIRELESS TELEPHONE OPERATES IN WINNIPEG

Dr. Lee De Forrest Gives Successful Demonstration of His Invention This Morning—Inventor Speaks With Mayor Evans

PITCHER AND OUTFIELDER JOIN THE MAROON CAMP

Rossbach and Isbell Arrive in City and Each "Looks" Like a Ball Player—Arrangements for Opening Ceremonies Under Way.

WILL PAVE SELKIRK AND WILLIAM AVES.

"Aldermen Must Get Together Before Other Improvements Are Ordered."

MILLIONS ED AT WEDDING

d Anthony J. Drexel—Invited for Days on Yachts and

TWENTY-FIVE MEN

Just as soon as they can practice at

De Forest himself claimed the trip was all business. He was visiting western Canada to determine the location of stations for his wireless system which would stretch from Chicago to points west. He prophesied that "in the near future" wireless would permit the distribution of the news of the country. Music, he said, would also be distributed by wireless; he told of an instance where a lady singing before a New York audience in one of the theatres was distinctly heard by wireless on the top of a neighbouring building. Wireless, he said, would permit a "wonderful development along these lines."

Business and civic leaders were charmed by the famous inventor as he spouted exactly what they wanted to hear. Winnipeg would be the centre of a wireless distribution system for the whole of Canada. His company would build a station, a factory and laboratory in the city. Nothing ever came of any of these ideas.

There were troubles for De Forest from the moment he stepped into the Royal Alexandra Hotel at Higgins and Main.

Some of the equipment he had shipped from New York was broken during the train trip. The inventor had hoped to demonstrate how sound could be transmitted without wires in both directions. The plan would now have to be scrapped. Transmission would only be one way.

Weather also became a factor. On April 15, Winnipeg was hit by a severe spring storm. It began as rain, turned to ice and then snow. One newspaper headline reported piercing sleet and gale force winds, with horse traffic at a standstill. Several horses had to be put down after falling on ice-covered roads. By Saturday, five inches of snow blanketed the city. Over a 36-hour period, the temperature dropped from 71 to 16 degrees Fahrenheit. The *Tribune* waxed eloquent about the early hours of the storm:

> "It did not take long after the precipitation began for every hole in the street and depression in the sidewalks to bear overwhelming testimony to the ability of the heavens to expose the imperfections of the works of man. There were puddles in abundance and miniature lakes inundating streets in various parts of the city. Citizens of whom it had been reported that they had not been known to swear for a very long time, permitted themselves to spoil a very excellent record by plunging into these pools and falling into profanity at one and the same time."

It is safe to assume that De Forest was among those cursing the elements. For his wireless demonstration to be successful, antennas had to be set up on top of Eaton's department store and the Royal Alexandra Hotel. Because of the weather, the work would not be done on schedule. De Forest's installations had to be delayed.

Finally, on Tuesday, April 19, all was in readiness. The temperature was warming after the storm as Winnipeggers flocked to Eaton's on Portage Avenue. Many, no doubt, stopped to look at the two flagpoles on top of the building with wires stretched between them. Among those in attendance that morning was the mayor of the city, Sanford Evans. Evans himself was no stranger to the communications business.

CHECKERS ON THE RADIO

"The first organization formed (in Winnipeg) for the pursuit of wireless investigation came in 1909. It was merely a group of enthusiasts who got together for discussions of common problems. Among the members were Mervin Sayer and Gordon Hignell, both of whom were killed in the war, Gordon Stovit, Alex Polson, and Gordon Struthers. They practised sending messages back and forth across the city with spark sets. The radiophone at that time had not been invented. Checker games by wireless were a popular pastime then, and members carried on such games from home to home."

Source: Winnipeg Tribune, April 20, 1922

He had founded the *Winnipeg Telegram* newspaper and had also set up a firm that provided news for the grain industry. On arrival at the department store, Evans was given a pair of makeshift headphones.

Back at the Royal Alexandra, De Forest was also busy. The moment of truth had arrived. As the *Tribune* explained, many people waiting at Eaton's were expecting the demonstration to be a flop. De Forest himself was unable to explain exactly how it all worked:

"The power which enabled this communication through space… was generated in a motor located in the hotel, whence it was carried into wires stretched between two flagpoles on the roof and thence expelled in some mysterious fashion."

Dr. Lee De Forest sat down before his wireless telephone and spoke into the contraption. Back at Eaton's, Mayor Evans was listening on his headphones. He heard the greetings "distinctly." Other receivers had been set up around the store, allowing a number of people to hear the voice of the inventor. Some described it as "weird", "supernatural" and "mysterious". Radio had arrived in western Canada.

Like the sound he transmitted, De Forest's promises of economic development for Winnipeg quickly disappeared into the ether. The demonstration did, however, have a lasting impact. It sparked a keen interest in wireless telephony. Most enthusiastic were the young. Students fascinated with the new technology took up the cause. By 1911, the Canadian Central Wireless Club was formed. It may have been the first of its kind in Canada. By 1913, the club reported 48 members. Other radio clubs popped up during the same period, experimenting with wireless. There was no formal programming, just static in the night and, at times, a few words here and there.

Early programming

Shortly before midnight on April 14, 1912, the passenger ship *Titanic* struck an iceberg and went down in the north Atlantic.

Winnipeg newspapers provided extensive coverage of the disaster. Among the stories was one on how wireless was helping to disseminate the latest information. Suddenly the potential of the new technology was front and centre for Winnipeggers desperate for information about what was happening at sea. "Interest in the disaster," according to one account, "has been evident in many directions but probably none so strikingly as the great crowds in front of the *Free Press* building all hours of the day and evening...people keen for the latest news as it trickled through its sources from the wireless instruments of the great liners out in the Atlantic."

Other events thousands of miles from home would also play a role in determining the future of radio in Manitoba. With the onset of World War I, the Canadian government banned all "amateur" and "non-essential" stations for security reasons. The move spelled an end to Winnipeg's Canadian Wireless Club, which disbanded. Overall, however, the war turned out to be a major boost for the new technology. The military trained many new men in the intricacies of wireless. Among the experimental stations established by the army was one in Brandon known as XWB. By 1918, with the surrender of Germany, wireless telephony had seen significant improvements. The ban was lifted and Manitoba was on the cusp of experiencing many radio firsts.

Kelvin Technical School had been built in 1912. Wireless became part of the curriculum and Kelvin became a hotbed for development of the new technology. A radio club was formed and soon there was a radio station, utilizing a war surplus transmitter with an antenna on the roof of the school. Amateur radio historian George Reynolds maintains that in the fall of 1921 Kelvin students provided Winnipeg residents with their first taste of music over the airwaves.

"Using an old-fashioned hand-wound Victrola and the club's only record, a well-scratched 78-rpm version of 'March of the Toreadors,' four club members would warm up the set and wind up the phonograph. One of them would hold the microphone in front of the horn of the Victrola while the rest would hurry home to listen to Bizet's music."

One year after Kelvin school opened, the Reverend George Salton packed up his belongings and moved his family from Moose Jaw to Winnipeg. They settled in a home at 1164 Grosvenor Avenue. George's son Lynn was a clever lad who had taken an interest in wireless while still in Moose Jaw. By the time he got to Winnipeg he was consumed with radio. The war intervened and Lynn signed on as a wireless operator for the Royal Navy. It was during his time serving in Gibraltar, the West Indies and at naval headquarters in London that he gained invaluable experience in wireless communications.

Upon returning to Winnipeg, Lynn Salton completed his studies at Wesley College. At age 23, he was appointed the first radio inspector for the prairies. His job was to ensure wireless radio operators obtained and paid for licences, regardless of whether they were sending or receiving signals. A year later, he set up the

Winnipeg first radio station CKZC was located in a home on Grosvenor Avenue. ANDY MOIR

Salton-Foster Radio Engineering Company at 294 Portage Avenue.

Not content to leave his work at the office, Salton conducted experiments at home on Grosvenor Avenue. He built a 100-watt transmitter at the house and began what would be Manitoba's first radio station. By this point, writes Reynolds, the province had "hundreds of wireless enthusiasts" that could potentially hear Salton's station that went by the call letters CKZC. He broadcast every Tuesday and Sunday night. "He had a good selection of phonograph records, his favourite being El Capitan March with which he began every broadcast." There was at least one report the station was heard more than 800 miles away. At age 25, young Salton had emerged as a radio boy wonder.

Newspapers of the air

Newspapers too were getting into the act. They viewed radio as a way to promote circulation.

Winnipeggers opening the *Free Press* on March 23, 1922 were informed the newspaper had been granted a license to operate a commercial radio station. Never before had the federal government authorized such a venture. The paper was bursting with enthusiasm for the new medium, noting that "thousands of amateurs throughout the continent are assisting in the exploitations of the radiophone and supplementing with new discoveries, a service the possibilities of which are so multifarious as to be almost unbelievable." For the masses who had difficulties with such eloquence, the *Free Press* promised the new radio station would provide "the finest information and music" with concerts, lectures and sermons.

Ten days later, at 10 pm, the ten-watt radio station went on the air with the ubiquitous Lynn Salton at the microphone. "Hello, hello, hello...*Free Press* broadcast number one." There were solos, speeches, orchestral numbers and even a prayer. The newspaper proclaimed the event a great success with an estimated 8,000 listeners. The accuracy of that number is highly debatable, given the very weak signal emanating from the *Free Press* building on Carlton Street. Still, by the *Free Press's* own account, "citizens from every part of the city telephoned their appreciation saying not a word or note was missed during the entire performance."

Only a few blocks away, the competing *Winnipeg Tribune* heaped scorn on *Free Press* radio, referring to it as the "Carlton Street peanut whistle." The *Tribune* had plans of its own for a bigger and more powerful radio station. The Marconi Company in Montreal had been commissioned to supply the latest equipment and engineering advice. The *Tribune* informed readers it was about to start "the first major broadcasting station in the prairie west."

A gala concert was planned for the grand opening of the new station, which went on the air April 20, 1922. The sixth floor of the *Tribune* building served as the studio for more than 200 performers. Over at the Fort Garry Hotel, a large audience waited in a ballroom to listen to the first program.

At 8 pm, CJNC *Tribune* radio went on the air with Lieutenant Governor Sir James Atkins presiding over the opening ceremonies. Among the highlights of the first night was the Princess Patricia band playing the "Colonel Bogey March" and the Winnipeg Oratorio Society singing the "Hallelujah Chorus." After all involved sang "God Save the King," the station signed off. CJNC was, however, back on the air the next night with baseball scores, news bulletins and music from gramophone records.

Like the *Free Press*, the *Tribune* was quick to call the venture a great success, reporting the station had been heard 773 miles away in Oshkosh, Wisconsin. "Letters and messages," noted the newspaper, "attest to the complete enjoyment of radio."

While listening may have been enjoyable, trying to get a radio receiver to function took some considerable effort. Crystal receivers required assembly. A significant part of the job was the erection of an aerial to catch incoming sound waves. "Amateurs installing a radio for the first time," advised the *Free Press*, "will find great care necessary, avoiding lining up of aerials parallel

WINNIPEG RADIO MAKES THE MOVIES

"It might be of interest to you that what was considered to be the first public broadcast in the world from a moving vehicle, took place in Canada...Early in May 1922 I put the Free Press' own station on the air and equipped my car with a portable broadcasting and receiving station. About a week later, still in May 1922, Miss Louise Lovely, a Hollywood Moving Picture Star, was making a personal appearance in Winnipeg and it was arranged that she would make this world's premier broadcast while I drove the car around the streets of Winnipeg. (There was a car in front and behind the moving radio station) that carried the Pathe and Fox newsreel cameramen respectively, who recorded the event which was shown to world-wide coverage."

Source: Letter written by Lynn V. Salton. Hammond Museum of Radio

to nearby telephone or telegraph wires, or crossing of wires in a receiving set."

A *Tribune* story in 1922 highlighted another hazard facing new radio owners. The aerials on top of buildings proved ideal conductors for lightning. "The subject of protection against lightning is the all absorbing topic among radio fans," declared the newspaper.

At age 89, former Winnipeg resident Art Webb remembered a telephone pole being whacked with an axe to try to get better radio reception. It was no doubt an act of frustration that played out more than once.

Despite technical challenges, radio was indeed breaking out all over. The most rapid growth was in the United States. The US Commerce Department reported that in 1921 there were 50,000 wireless telephones, as they were then known. By 1922, the number had increased to 600,000. KDKA in Pittsburgh had been providing regular programming since 1920. Stations in other American cities were now on the air.

In Canada, the Marconi Company decided the best way to sell radio receivers was to provide programming for people to listen to. An engineer named Darby Coats helped set up a Marconi station in Montreal known as XWA. Coats would eventually become a key player in the development of radio and television in Manitoba.

The rapidly emerging technology did not go unnoticed by the business community. Eaton's established a radio department at its Winnipeg store in 1922. Lynn V. Salton was hired to run the department. He moved station CJZC from his Grosvenor Avenue home to the fourth floor of Eaton's, where he could provide demonstrations on how radio worked. Crystal receiving sets sold for $15 without headphones. Federal receiving sets were $35 with phones. Hemphill Trade School at 209 Pacific Avenue began classes on installing most radio equipment. Several other businesses in the city were now also selling radios.

Theatre broadcasts

Even theatres got into the act. The Capitol and Allen (later Metropolitan) offered the equivalent of radio and a movie. Both theatres claimed to be the first in Canada to provide such entertainment. The Allen boasted it had installed the largest receiving set in western Canada and promised messages from Wales, France and Germany, with music from New York, Boston, Pittsburgh and San Francisco. The obvious preference for non-Canadian programs would emerge as a major broadcasting issue in years to come.

On the evening of July 18, 1922, hundreds of Winnipeggers flocked to the Lyceum and College theatres. It wasn't the latest Charlie Chaplin film that was scheduled for the silver screen that night. Rather the patrons had come to hear provincial election results on radio. The stations operated by the *Free Press* and *Tribune* were both offering election coverage. Since relatively few Winnipeggers owned receiving sets, the theatres set up equipment allowing the public to listen to the returns as they wafted magically over the airwaves.

Based on newspaper accounts, the broadcasts were a success. The *Free Press* offered bulletins throughout the evening. The more powerful *Tribune* station "maintained continuous transmission service from 5:20 pm until 11 o'clock." The length of the broadcast itself was no small feat. Up until that time, the stations rarely stayed on the air more than a couple of hours. "During (intervals between) returns interest was kept up by musical selections on the latest gramophone records."

Towards the end of the evening, successful independent Labour candidate Fred J. Dixon showed up at the *Tribune* building and "gave a brief address to electors over the *Tribune* radiophone." Forever after, politicians would scramble to be heard over the broadcast airwaves.

The *Tribune* broadcast was heard as far away as Manitou and Grandview. A Winnipeg judge called the *Tribune* to report "he had heard everything with distinction and he considered the service all that could be desired."

The election turned out to be historic as the United Farmers swept to power, catapulting John Bracken to the Premier's chair... a position he would hold for 21 years. It was also a monumental night for broadcasting, in that it was the first time in the nation's history that radio had provided full coverage of a major news event. Only a few months earlier, the *Free Press* station had made sports history by being the first radio station in Canada to broadcast a hockey game in its entirety.

Radio in Manitoba was on its way, although no one, as yet, was exactly sure where it was going.

"C.N.R.W."
BROADCASTING STUDIO
FORT GARRY HOTEL
WINNIPEG CANADA

CHAPTER TWO

Radio In a Tuxedo

At the Winnipeg Grain Exchange, grain barons were grumbling about rising telephone costs to keep elevator agents informed on latest market trends. By the early 1920s, the Exchange was paying close to $100,000 a year to the Manitoba Telephone System, an outrageous sum in the minds of certain grain merchants. Was there not a cheaper way? Then someone hit on an idea that would potentially eliminate telephone calls altogether. It was called radio.

The rumblings at the Grain Exchange were worrying John E. Lowry, the Commissioner of Telephones. Only a year earlier, he had taken on the top job at the financially shaky MTS. In 1921, the number of telephone subscribers in rural Manitoba was actually declining. Now came the possibility that a huge piece of business might be eliminated because of this new technology called radio. "It is easy to see," wrote Lowry to the Minister of Telephones, "where we might lose a lot of revenue."

While the Commissioner of Telephones was worried about losing revenue to radio, executives at the *Free Press* and the *Tribune* were more concerned about generating revenue with radio. The stations they had started turned out to be time consuming, labor intensive and expensive to operate. They had hoped radio programming would boost newspaper circulation, but that hadn't really materialized. As companies in such circumstances often do, they looked to the government for help... specifically the Manitoba Telephone System. Exactly who approached whom first is a matter of conjecture. There is evidence that Commissioner Lowry was quite receptive to the idea that the telephone company start its own radio station. The government even had a 100-watt transmitter ready for use. Somewhere around 1920, MTS had purchased the equipment for an experimental project to send messages to The Pas. The experiment never worked out and the transmitter had been left sitting in an old

Opposite: Herb Roberts (in tuxedo) at CNRW studio in Fort Garry Hotel. MANITOBA ARCHIVES

CKY
WINNIPEG MANITOBA

D.R.P. COATS
Mngr Radio Dept
Announcer at CKY

LILLIAN SHAW
Stenographer and
Assistant Announcer

WILLIAM DUFFIELD
Operator in Charge
of Equipment

RADIO STATION
CKY

EDWARD DUSANG
Assistant Operator

MANITOBA'S OWN STATION

shed. Lowry was determined it would not go to waste.

In January of 1923, top executives from the Winnipeg dailies struck a deal with the Manitoba Telephone System. The newspapers would get out of the radio business. MTS would take over, operating a government-owned radio station to be called CKY.

The formation of CKY was historic on several fronts. The enterprise would be the first publicly owned radio station in Canada. Equally remarkable was the agreement Manitoba was able to reach with federal authorities over control of the airwaves. While Ottawa would technically retain jurisdiction over licensing, it was agreed that no new station could be approved without the consent of the Manitoba Telephone System. The deal gave MTS massive power over the development of radio in the province. In years to come, the Commissioner of Telephones would do all in his power to ensure there would be very little competition for CKY.

A second provision involved money. Anyone who owned a radio receiver in the

Early CKY staff and MTS building on Sherbrook.
HERB ROBERTS SCRAPBOOK

1920s was expected to pay a one-dollar license fee to the federal government. Under the agreement, fifty cents of every dollar collected in Manitoba would go to support CKY.

Few broadcast executives have wielded the power of John E. Lowry. A hard-drinking Irishman, he was trained as an electrical engineer and emigrated to Canada in 1908 to oversee the automation of Edmonton's telephone service. By the time he took over as head of the Manitoba Government Telephones in 1921, he had a track record as a man who could get things done. He was energetic, sometimes autocratic, and if things did not go his way, he didn't always play by the rules. At the same time he was working to establish CKY, Lowry was hauled into court for failing to comply with an order from the Provincial Utilities Commission. The agency had concluded that some residents of East Kildonan had been wronged by the Telephone System and should receive a reduction in their telephone bills. After meeting with a group of concerned politicians, Lowry reportedly said he "would pay no attention to the order,

the existing rates would remain in force and no refunds would be made." The matter was eventually resolved, but the case serves as an example of how obstinate the Telephone Commissioner could be.

Winnipeggers opening their daily newspapers on March 8 were informed the government telephone system would assume control of all radio in Manitoba. "We do not wish to convey," declared a *Tribune* executive, "that Manitoba Government Telephones has forced us out of radio broadcasting." In fact, the *Tribune* concluded, many listeners would be happy to see the newspapers out of the radio business. "We have had many complaints that the Winnipeg stations hogged the ether so much that it has been difficult to listen to broadcasting stations in other parts of Canada and in the United States. We believe Manitoba Telephones will be merciful."

CKY radio officially went on the air March 13, 1923. The transmitter was located on the roof of the Manitoba Government Telephone building at 297 Sherbrook Street. The studio and offices

were combined in a single floor below. Listeners could hear the 500-watt station at 665 on the dial. Compared to previous grand openings in the city, the launch of CKY was a low-key affair. Premier John Bracken promised the Telephone System would put radio on "a revenue earning basis as far as possible and develop it as a public utility for entertainment, instructional and commercial use." The premier called on local musicians and music lovers to co-operate with Manitoba Telephones in securing talent to provide programs (translate: work for free). In keeping with the frugal nature of the evening, no expensive outside talent was brought in for the inaugural program. Among the highlights...a soprano solo by a Miss Johnson, while Mr. Duff offered up imitation bird calls. The evening was capped off by the Telephone Male Choir with its rendition of "Old Virginny and Kentucky Babe." Public radio had arrived.

CKY was on the air an hour and 15 minutes every day except Sunday. Three times a week, the station was heard for two hours in the evening. On Sunday evenings, there

was a church service if available. Otherwise there was a concert of sacred music.

While programming in the evening was usually live, daytime programs consisted of phonograph records, news items and market reports. Listeners could tune in for favourites of the day such as "I Love Me, Oh Harold, and Barney Google." Writing in the MTS publication *Manitoba Calling*, one radio veteran recalled that "music was broadcast by standing a microphone in front of a phonograph. The phonographs themselves were operated with a clockwork system. As the clockwork mechanism ran down, the voices of entertainers would go slower and slower, causing some listeners to complain."

The task of keeping CKY on the air fell on the shoulders of one Douglas Richard Proctor Coats, better known as Darby. At the new radio station, Coats was Mr. Everything. He served as manager, announcer, engineer and probably even janitor. Over the next forty years, Coats would become a household name in the province. If a case were to be made for a "father of

radio" in Manitoba, it would surely be Darby Coats.

As a youngster growing up in Gravesend, England, near London, Darby was known as "the Drip" because of his initials D.R.P. He was keenly interested in astronomy and the new technology known as wireless. He attended the British School of Telegraphy, and at age 17, built his first radio receiver, using a kite as the antenna. The goal was to pick up Morse code signals from Paris or some other faraway location.

After immigrating to Canada at age 19, Coats took to the sea, becoming a wireless operator for the Marconi Company. The job nearly led to his demise. On two separate occasions, ships on which he was working ran into trouble. He sent out his first S.O.S. when the *S.S. City of Sydney* ran aground on rocks near Sambro, Nova Scotia. More frightening was an event which occurred during World War I. Coats was a telegraph operator on the *S.S Morewenna* when the ship was torpedoed by a German submarine in May 1915.

Opposite: "Darby Coats" (wearing headphones) helps boxing champ Jack Dempsey through a broadcast. CKSB COLLECTION. LA SOCIETE HISTORIQUE DE SAINT-BONIFACE

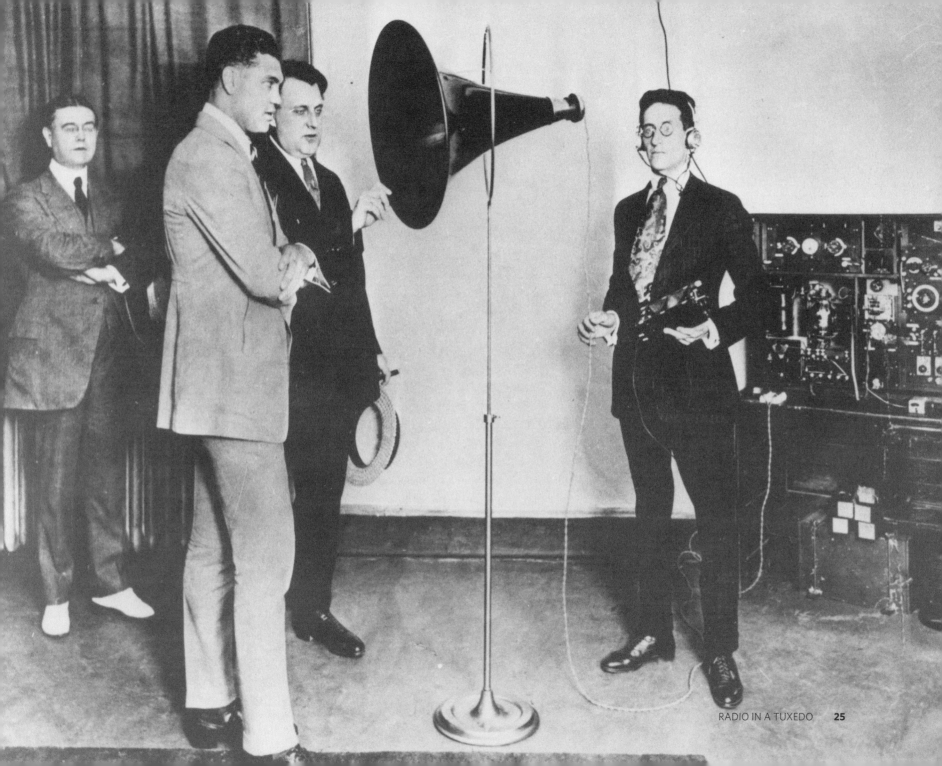

Safely back on dry land, Darby Coats made broadcasting history when he played a role in getting Marconi radio station XWA on the air. He liked to tell the story of the first music played on the Montreal station. After getting tired of counting or reading the alphabet to test sound equipment, the engineers got the bright idea of borrowing records from a nearby Montreal record shop. Coats would collect the records and then mention the name of the store when the music was played over the airwaves. On December 18, 1919, Coats was at the controls and on the air as experimental programming got underway. Six months later, regular programming commenced, launching what many argue was the first commercial radio station in the world.

During his time in Montreal, Coats could also lay claim to taking a poke, or at least a shove, at world heavyweight boxing champion Jack Dempsey. The champion had arrived at the radio station to promote an upcoming exhibition match. Coats assumed the man who could pack such a powerful punch would also have a powerful voice.

"I therefore placed him back from the wide end of the horn (microphone). He surprised me however by speaking with a very small voice, by no means helped by the nervousness he was suffering. The pugilist was letting me down. He must move closer to the microphone but he was too absorbed in his script to see my signals...so I shoved Mr. Dempsey in the back hoping he would not misunderstand. It was the only time I pushed a heavyweight champion around. When Jack finished his address he spoke to me and said 'Gee, I'd rather fight ten fights than do that again.'"

Cupid and the call of the west struck at almost the same time for Darby Coats. He had met a girl from Longueuil named Amy Cooper. She was six years younger and captured his heart. During the same period, Coats received a job offer to sell radio equipment for Perkins Electric in Winnipeg. There was the potential to make good money. Coats decided to head west, but not without the love of his life. Darby

and Amy were married on August 19, 1922 in Longueuil. The same day, they boarded a train for Winnipeg.

It turned out Darby wasn't much of a salesman. In the words of his son Jim, "he would sooner give everything away." When the job of managing CKY came up, Coats jumped at the opportunity. It was the start of a career that made him a local, and to some extent national, celebrity.

The biggest challenge for the new recruit was to find programming for CKY. Daytime broadcasts consisted of news items read directly from newspapers, market reports and phonograph records. Coats saw radio as an educational tool, and his programming reflected that. Listeners were treated to academics speaking on such topics as "Modern Ideas and Electricity" and "Teeth and Health." The Agricultural College provided lectures for farmers and there were lessons in Esperanto. Local churches were ecstatic to be able to deliver their message over the air. One preacher claimed no less than three conversions in one weekend.

According to the MTS publication *Manitoba Calling*, the lot of the lone CKY staffer was not easy:

"The manager and announcer had to telephone dozens of artists each day in the hope of persuading some to assist in forthcoming broadcasts. He attended to fan mail which was often a day's work in itself. He had to select phonograph records from local stores, interview visitors and copy all the grain markets by telephone, often performing this duty while playing records on the air. If a record finished while he was receiving the reports he had to ask the person dictating at the other end of the telephones to excuse him. Then he changed the record and needle, wound the machine and settled himself again to the task of writing the prices of wheat and barley."

While CKY was a publicly owned station, performers on the radio would receive none of the benefits of a civil servant. Singers, musicians and other entertainers were expected to work free of charge. The programming day was often determined by the order in which the acts arrived. Quality control was unheard of. According to one MTS account, there was once an opera singer who "had taken excessively of hot weather refreshment" prior to her appearance. "She stood unsteadily by the piano and insisted on hiccoughing the *Star of Eve* until she was persuaded to leave quietly." It would not be the last time an inebriated broadcaster was heard over the Manitoba airwaves.

Making airtime available to Members of Parliament, MLAs and city councillors was also a cheap and easy way to fill time, although it rarely made for the most entertaining programming. For publicly-owned CKY there was the obvious danger of the station being perceived as an arm of the governing party. One of the early decisions set out by manager Coats dealt with the issue. In an unpublished manuscript cited by historian Mary Vipond, Coats explained his policy:

"CKY's microphone must be available to all political parties on the basis of equal time and payment...on the day prior to an election free and equal time would be allowed each of the local candidates to state his or her platform in a period to be arranged. The order of introduction at the microphone would be that in which the candidates arrived at the studio."

This was almost certainly the first attempt by a broadcaster to spell out some basic journalistic policy.

Generating revenue was another challenge. Premier Bracken had served notice from day one that the radio station was at least expected to break even. In this regard, the Manitoba Telephone System was able to use its monopoly power to attract a substantial source of funding. The cash came from the Canadian National Railway.

Railway Radio

In the early 1920s, CNR President Sir Henry Thornton hatched a plan he was convinced would bring more passengers on board his trains. The idea was to put radio receivers in rail cars so that passengers

First broadcast on CNRW enjoyed by Prince of Wales.
HERB ROBERTS SCRAPBOOK

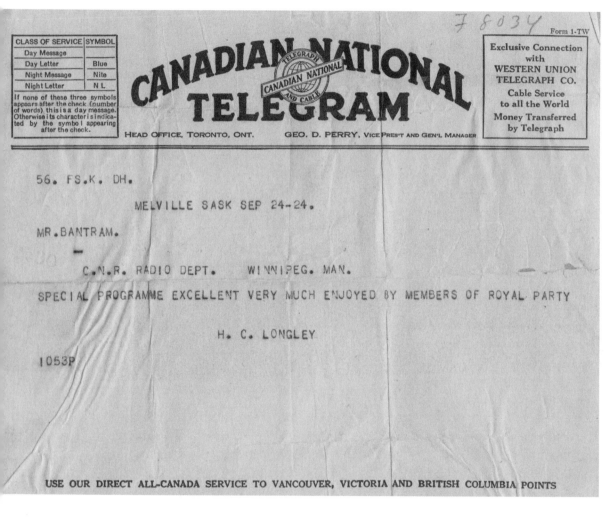

could be entertained while they travelled. The programming would be provided by a series of radio stations built in major cities across the country. CNR was quickly granted licenses for stations in Ottawa, Montreal and Vancouver. When it came to Winnipeg, it was a different story. John Lowry and the Manitoba Telephone System were not about to permit another station to compete with CKY. Instead, they agreed to lease time on CKY for CNR broadcasts. In July of 1924, the new Winnipeg station was granted the call letters CNRW. It was commonly known as a "phantom station" because it had no transmitter.

Few broadcasters begin their careers programming to royalty, but that was the case for Herb Roberts at CNRW. On his first day on the job in 1924, he hosted a program of mostly music to the Royal Train carrying the Prince of Wales to a ranch in Alberta. Soon after, Roberts received a telegram saying the "royal party enjoyed the program very much."

CNR's Fort Garry Hotel served as headquarters for CNRW Winnipeg.

The railway company made considerable effort to provide varied and quality programming. Virtually all of the hotel programs were live, with the house orchestra a ready source of entertainment. On Saturday nights, there was a supper dance broadcast. On Sunday, it was "Evening Musical" from the mezzanine of the Fort Garry.

At the microphone for each of these events was the immaculately clad Herb Roberts. For Canadian National, radio broadcasting was a high-class undertaking. It was radio in a tuxedo, and the bespectacled young Roberts with his mellifluous tones and Welsh accent personified the era. "I changed into my tuxedo for every broadcast," recalled Roberts during an interview later in life. "It was just the proper thing to do."

Roberts was also an innovator in that he was one of the early announcers to incorporate sound into his broadcasts. As he was representing the railway, he obtained an old train bell which was installed in the Fort Garry studio. When a broadcast on CNRW was about to begin, Roberts would ring the train bell while his secretary would rub two pieces of sandpaper together. The effect was the sound of a train starting up. It became a regular theme for the radio station.

During the 1920s, CNR pumped considerable sums into Canada's first radio network. Programming from Winnipeg was appearing regularly on the network, while local residents could listen to programs originating from other cities on the CNR line. In an article marking the station's fifth anniversary, the *Free Press* gushed over the radio station, noting that "Irvin Plum's Jasper Park Lodge Orchestra broadcasting dinner and dance programs from the (Fort Garry) hotel has made itself popular throughout the west.... some of the city's most popular soloists have been given wider audiences by beans (sic) of CNRW."

One of the more unique pieces of programming done out of Winnipeg was a broadcast in 1929 featuring an aboriginal band from the United States. The group, known as the United States Indian Band, had played at the inauguration of President Hoover and was visiting Winnipeg. The CNRW program was only the group's second appearance on radio and featured a selection of "Indian melodies, a few popular numbers, and individual solos by some members of the orchestra."

On July 1, 1927, Canada celebrated its Diamond Jubilee. As the bells rang out from the newly installed Carillon on Parliament Hill, Canadians listened from coast to coast. It was the first nationwide radio broadcast, and CNR radio played an instrumental role in ensuring the programming was a success.

Another significant undertaking by Canadian National was to bring renowned British director Tyrone Guthrie from England to write and produce a series of radio plays, known as "The Romance of Canada." These received critical acclaim and proved popular. Among the dramas was the story of the Selkirk settlers arriving in Manitoba. "For about 20 weeks we churned out a new historical episode every Tuesday," wrote Guthrie in a theatrical notebook, "often with large casts and complicated 'effects'. The Romance of Canada fell sick of a disease to which all serial undertakings are liable: the gradual exhaustion of the author."

"LIKE HELL HE IS"

Early radio was perceived as a high-class venture, and the slightest on-air indiscretion could get one fired. Not that it didn't happen.

Herb Roberts, the first announcer on CNRW radio, was given the challenge of broadcasting play-by-play curling at the Granite curling club in Winnipeg. Roberts stood amongst a large crowd of spectators and worked his way through the broadcast. With a flair for the dramatic, Roberts described the final shot which would determine the outcome of the championship game: "The skip is in the hack, he polishes his rock, it's on its way, it's halfway down the ice. It's going to be close. I think he's going to miss it. I think he's going to miss it."

A nearby fan could not take it any longer. "Like hell it is," he pronounced loudly, no doubt to the horror of Roberts and at least some of his listeners.

What was said at the curling rink was mild however, compared to what listeners heard during a speech by the president of Canadian National Railway. Sir Henry Thornton was well into his address when suddenly the airwaves turned blue with some of the strongest expletives one could utter. CNR engineers were frantic until it was determined the source was a worker at the Sprague subdivision in southeastern Manitoba. Apparently the man had accidentally tapped into the broadcast line. The employee was under the impression he was talking to a work train that was shutting down for the night.

Having to share a transmitter with CKY meant CNRW was on the air only a few hours a week. For CKY, it meant a steady source of income. By 1929, the "phantom station" was paying the Manitoba Telephone System over $14,000 a year to rent the CKY facilities. The MTS station was also collecting a 50-cent licensing fee from supposedly everyone who owned a radio. By 1928, the number of receivers licensed in Manitoba topped 20,000. Technically, advertising was not permitted but Commissioner Lowry had lobbied hard and some CKY programming was being sponsored. According to the Canadian Communications Foundation, one of the first advertisers was the J.J.H. Maclean piano company.

Some businesses were actually providing programming to the Manitoba government station. The Hudson's Bay store, built in 1926, had its own radio show with store staff providing the talent. The purpose of the exercise was to sell radios. A 1928 article in the *Free Press* noted "the development of the Hudson's Bay Company radio business is going forward rapidly... officials attribute part of the success to the company's regular weekly musical programmes which are put on the air over CKY."

There is little argument that one of the reasons for CKY's success was its monopoly. While private radio stations were popping up in other parts of the country, MTS rejected all proposals for new radio services in Manitoba. Not that CKY was totally without competition. Manitobans loved listening to American radio and there was plenty to choose from. As early as 1924, Winnipeg newspapers were listing programming from no less than 25 US stations. Boxing was extremely popular. Heavyweight championship fights between Jack Dempsey and Gene Tunney broadcast on American radio drew large audiences in Manitoba. There were also occasions when CKY actually picked up and rebroadcast American programs.

Competition

No doubt sensing the commercial possibilities of radio, James Richardson and Sons Limited made the first serious challenge to the Manitoba government's radio monopoly. The grain merchant had already established a radio station in Moose Jaw to broadcast commodity prices to local farmers and elevator agents. With an offer of better pay, the company even lured Darby Coats away from Winnipeg to run the Moose Jaw operation. The Richardsons hoped to expand their business into Manitoba and requested a licence to set up a station in Brandon. Rural residents in that part of the province had long complained about poor reception of CKY programming. MTS did not deny there was a problem but placed the blame squarely on the Americans, claiming US signals were drowning out CKY. Commissioner Lowry fired off an angry letter to Ottawa, demanding the federal government take action to deal with the Americans. In classic overstatement, Lowry complained the situation was "getting

steadily worse until now it appears almost a waste of time, effort and money to put a good program on the air from our station."

MTS was in no mood for competition from the Richardsons or anyone else. Lowry exercised the province's veto, concluding it was not in the public interest for another radio station to be established in the province. The Richardsons fought back, with company president James Armstrong Richardson going directly to Premier Bracken to state his case. The plea fell on deaf ears.

The fact remained, however, that many parts of southwestern Manitoba had reception problems. Brandon was growing rapidly and the wheat economy was strong. Pressure mounted. The Bracken government, whose power base was rural Manitoba, could not ignore the calls for better radio. MTS came up with a scheme that would see CKY boost its power with a new 5,000-watt transmitter to be located at the Manitoba Agricultural College, which is now part of the University of Manitoba. CKY's old transmitter would then be

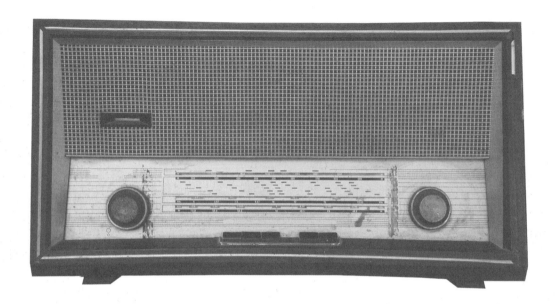

moved to Brandon and the wheat city would have its own radio station, owned and operated by the Manitoba Telephone System. There was only one catch. MTS proposed that Brandon should pay a $4,500 annual fee for the privilege of having its own radio station. City fathers were not amused.

In the midst of all this, the Richardsons played a final card that left John Lowry and the Telephone System crying foul. The grain company applied for and received a licence to operate a radio station in Fleming, Saskatchewan, only three miles from the Manitoba border. Studios would be located at the Royal Alexandra Hotel in Winnipeg. Grain prices and programming would be sent via CP telegraph lines to the Fleming transmitter and then sent over the airwaves back into Manitoba. MTS protested vehemently, but federal officials insisted there was nothing they could do. For the first time, CKY would have a private sector competitor.

The Richardson's new radio station, with the call letters CJRW, went on the air in September 1928. The 85-foot towers were mounted with 500-watt lamps, which, according to newspaper accounts, were "visible at night for many miles across the prairie." Programming came from both Moose Jaw and Winnipeg. One of the station's first announcers was Tony Messenger who did a program "about furs and fur bearing animals and trapping." Another early CJRW broadcaster was Les Garside, who recalled that his new boss, Dawson Richardson, refused to allow any pre-recorded programming. Everything was to be done live. CJRW discovered fairly quickly that live on-location radio did have its limitations. Initially, the station provided market reports directly from the pit of the trading floor at Winnipeg Grain Exchange. "The language was so bad they had to stop," said Garside.

CKY was not to be outdone. That fall, what was described as a new CKY went on the air with a 5,000-watt transmitter, making it the most powerful radio station in the country. "It is the best station in the Dominion, and no station outside Canada has more modern equipment," crowed Lowry. Premier Bracken used the opportunity to talk about CKY's financial success, noting that the station had been self-supporting for the last four years, and that the new CKY should improve rural service.

By December, the old CKY transmitter and towers had found a new home on the grounds of Brandon City Hall. Civic leaders had finally worked out a compromise with MTS. In addition to providing a location for the new station transmitter, the city also agreed to provide light, heat and power. On December 11, 1928, CKX radio went on the air. The station still had no announcer. Most of what would be heard on CKX would be programs from CKY in Winnipeg. CKY announcer F.P. Rutland did travel to Brandon for an opening program, which consisted of speeches, songs

HOCKEY HISTORY— RADIO MYSTERY

"Stephenson shoots.... blocked by the Port Arthur keeper."

We can only speculate as to the exact words, but on February 22, 1923, radio and hockey history was made at the Winnipeg Amphitheatre. On that night, for the first time, a hockey game was broadcast in its entirety. The match was between the Olympic champion Winnipeg Falcons and the Port Arthur Bearcats.

Only 14 days earlier, Toronto sports reporter Norman Albert provided play-by-play of the third period of an amateur game in Toronto. The broadcast on station CFCA was the first play-by-play hockey heard on radio. A week later, the same station broadcast the final period of an NHL game between Toronto St. Pats and Ottawa.

The Winnipeg game had generated huge interest and because many people could not get tickets, *Free Press* radio station CJCG decided to broadcast the action from start to finish. "The popularity of the service which enabled the many who were unable to attend the game to keep posted on the entire play as fast as it took place was shown by enthusiastic reports from city and outside points from listeners," declared the *Free Press* in a report on the game the following day.

One of the most intriguing aspects of the broadcast is the name of the play-by-play announcer. It is never given in any newspaper accounts. According to one article the job was handled by the sporting editor of the *Free Press*. At the time, the sports editor of the paper was W.J. Billy Finlay, a noted lacrosse player and curler. In the past, he had covered numerous Falcon games, so it is plausible he would be a likely candidate; but whether it was Finlay who handled the job has never been completely corroborated.

First CKX tower located at Brandon City Hall.
S.J. MCKEE ARCHIVES BRANDON

and orchestral music. Brandonites who did not own a radio could still hear the opening ceremonies at St. Paul's United Church or at the city hall auditorium. According to at least one source, a portion of the programming on opening day apparently wasn't fit to be heard in church, and some censorship was required. A *Brandon Sun* article noted "the medium was silenced during the offerings of The Goblins Orchestra whose tapping renditions of 'She Didn't Say Yes, She Didn't Say No' and other tunes only reached listeners out of town." Initially, CKX radio was on the air Thursday, Friday and Sunday evenings from eight-thirty to ten o'clock.

As the "roaring twenties" drew to a close, it was evident radio was more than just a passing fad. In only a few years the medium had become an important source of information and entertainment, not only locally but across North America. It was hardly cheap entertainment. The cost of a "radio receiver" at stores in Winnipeg ranged from $75 to over $200. Despite the cost, the number of radios owned and licensed in Manitoba increased from 632 in 1922 to over 20,000 in 1929. Even this number is probably low, as it is virtually certain some people had radios but did not bother to pay the one-dollar licence fee.

Technological breakthroughs had also advanced the medium. Toronto inventor and entrepreneur, Edward Samuel "Ted" Rogers, had developed a radio tube that would operate on an alternating current. No longer did a radio require huge and expensive batteries. It could simply be plugged in. By the mid-twenties, battery-less radios were the latest product in a growing market. Radios were being advertised not just for their entertainment and information value, but also as a piece of decorative living room furniture.

The future indeed looked bright. Yet no one in broadcasting, or elsewhere, had any idea of the seismic economic shift just around the corner. Radio would be affected in unexpected ways.

CHAPTER THREE

Dust Storms, Teepee Tales, and Radio Fit For a King

No one can fully define what radio meant for those who lived through the Depression on the Canadian prairies. It was many things...a form of escapism, a focal point for neighbourly gatherings, an instrument for social change and, most of all, a shared experience.

"Radio listening was a passion that the unemployed shared with the employed, the rich shared with the poor," wrote historian and journalist James Gray, in documenting his own experiences in Winnipeg during the dirty thirties. "Radio was not only entertainment, it enabled farm people to shut themselves away from the depression itself, from the dust and from the wind that blew night and day with its incessant, deranging whine."

Even before the stock market crash of 1929 the winds of change were beginning to blow for Canadian radio. The emerging issues were hardly insignificant. Because radio listening was a "shared experience," the medium had become a force in shaping public opinion. Who should control radio? Should there be restrictions to access? Should radio be the domain of the public sector or commercial interests? The answers to these questions would have a dramatic impact on Manitoba radio before the decade was out.

By the late 1920s, church services and religious programming were standard fare on most Canadian stations. CKY alone claimed to have 15 telephone lines from churches for Sunday evening broadcasts. None of this stirred the slightest controversy until the arrival of an organization known as the Bible Students' Association...an arm of the Jehovah Witnesses. The Bible Students

Opposite: CKY truck 1932.
WESTERN CANADA PICTORIAL INDEX.

managed to set up four radio stations in other parts of the country and touched off a firestorm with vitriolic attacks on the national government and the Catholic Church. In his book "Coast to Coast," broadcaster Sandy Stewart provided an excerpt from one such broadcast:

> "That wicked organization (The Catholic Church) acting under the pretext of being God's representative on this earth, has crushed every organization that has ever risen against it. Now Christ is on his throne and God's time has come to put his kingdom completely in control under Christ, the Roman Catholic hierarchy has begun and carries on its assaults against God's true people."

Making matters worse, the Ku Klux Klan was airing a program on a Saskatchewan station under the guise of religious programming. Describing such programs as "unpatriotic and abusive of all our churches," the federal cabinet minister responsible for radio licensing took action and shut down the four stations operated by the Bible Students. What ensued was a political brouhaha, with Winnipeg Labour Member of Parliament J.S. Woodsworth accusing the government of censorship. The controversy over the Bible Students' Association, coupled with mounting concern over the dominance of American radio in Canada, prompted the government of Mackenzie King to set up a Royal Commission to make recommendations on the future of radio broadcasting in Canada.

The Commission was headed by John Aird, chairman of the Canadian Bank of Commerce. The question to be answered, as set out by the federal government, was straightforward: should radio in Canada be owned and operated by the national government, the private sector or provincial governments?

The Aird Commission began its work by visiting New York and London. The United States had left radio to the private sector. In Britain, broadcasting was a totally public enterprise, with radio stations owned and operated by the British Broadcasting Corporation. Over the next two months, the commissioners also visited 25 Canadian cities to sound out public opinion.

The people who showed up for hearings in Brandon and Winnipeg made it clear they didn't think much of Manitoba Government radio. CKX and CKY came in for a barrage of criticism. Although CKX had been on the air for only a few months, there were complaints about the quality of local content. The president of the Brandon Board of Trade told the commissioners "in so far as the local situation is concerned, they could do a far better class of programming." When Aird and his group arrived at the Manitoba Legislature the next day, they heard complaints that CKY was interfering with other stations since it boosted its power in 1928. Darby Coats, now firmly entrenched with the Richardsons in the private sector, said if Canada went to a system of public radio he would be on the train for the United States. In an editorial, a few days after the Commissioners departed, the *Free Press* concluded that CKY had received what it called "the razz."

Less than two months after public hearings ended, the Aird Commission submitted its report. Although only nine pages in length, the recommendations were sweeping and would shape the nature of radio broadcasting in Canada for decades to come. What the commission proposed was a national broadcasting system, owned and operated by the federal government. The nation would be served by seven high-powered radio stations. The Commission went so far as to suggest there be no commercial radio in Canada. Existing private stations would be closed or purchased by the new national broadcasting agency, to be known as the Canadian Radio Broadcasting Commission.

Immediate reaction from the Manitoba Telephone System was surprisingly muted. Perhaps this was because the Commission had also suggested that representatives from each province would be responsible for programming in their own areas. John Lowry and other Manitoba officials would have recognized immediately that the proposals would have far-reaching implications for CKY, CKX and the MTS monopoly.

The report sent a chill through private broadcasters, but there would be no immediate action from the governing Liberals. Only five weeks after the report's submission, the stock market crashed and politicians faced more pressing issues. The economic situation and political turmoil saw the King government turfed from office in the 1930 election. The new Conservative Prime Minister, R.B. Bennett, would have to decide what to do with the Aird report.

Mr. Bennett had no shortage of advice to draw from. Representing private interests was the newly formed Canadian Association of Broadcasters, of which CKY was a member. By far, the more effective lobby proved to be an organization known as the Canadian Radio League. The league was headed by two devout Canadian nationalists named Graham Spry and Allan Plaunt. Spry, a Rhodes Scholar, had received his Bachelor of Arts degree at the University of Manitoba and, before graduation, was hired on at the *Free Press*. There he was mentored by legendary *Free Press* editor and unabashed Liberal John Dafoe. Both Spry

and Plaunt knew their way around corridors of power, and the Canadian Radio League used every opportunity to promote the central features of the Aird report. "Goodness knows we lobbied," recalled Spry in a CBC interview, "We went to see every Member of Parliament, every senator, and above all every cabinet minister we could possibly see." Spry even went so far as to study the daily habits of the prime minister. "If I wanted to get something through to him I would run into him by 'accident' just as he was going to have his massage in the swimming pool at the Chateau Laurier."

At the same time, the Depression was taking a heavy toll on the operations of the Canadian National Railway. CNR management had come in for sharp criticism from some Conservative politicians who held up the radio division as but one example of profligate spending by the crown corporation.

Finally, in 1932, the Bennett administration unveiled its new broadcast policy. To a significant degree, the Conservatives accepted the recommendations of the

Aird report. Canada would have a national broadcasting system, operated by an organization known as the Canadian Radio Broadcasting Commission. It would be funded by the national government, license fees and advertising. Provincial representatives would have a say over programming in their own regions. Private stations would serve as affiliates of the new national agency.

For broadcasters in Manitoba, the decision was monumental. With the stroke of a pen in Ottawa, MTS lost its radio monopoly with the formation of the Canadian Radio Broadcasting Commission. CNRW was also gone, as one of the first acts of CRBC was to purchase CNR radio stations and equipment to develop its own cross country system. CKY and CKX continued to operate as provincially owned radio stations, renting some programming time to the new national agency. With the MTS monopoly gone, James Richardson and Sons soon applied for and received a license for a station in Winnipeg. The company already had studios in the Royal

Alexandra Hotel, and the new station, with the call letters CJRC, went on the air in January 1934.

The Manitoba government hardly gave up without a fight. Led by Quebec, a number of provinces, including Manitoba, took to the courts, challenging the federal government's exclusive jurisdiction over broadcasting. The drawn-out legal battle was finally settled in London with the British Privy Council rejecting the arguments of Manitoba and the other provinces. From that day forth, broadcasting would remain the responsibility of the federal government.

As it turned out, the Canadian Radio Broadcasting Commission had a short life. From day one, controversy swirled around the new broadcasting agency. Financing was an issue. Canadians didn't much like the increased two-dollar license fee being used to fund the Commission. Even so, the CRBC's budget was considerably smaller than what had been recommended by Aird. The Radio League complained long and loudly about the slow development of new Canadian programming.

Then came the infamous "Mr. Sage"...a tiny radio soap opera that ultimately spelled doom for the CRBC. "Mr. Sage" was a friendly chap who would wax eloquent on things political. He just happened to pop up on the radio during the 1935 election campaign, with no apparent purpose other than to bash the Liberals and their leader Mackenzie King. During the 15-minute programs, Mr. Sage accused the Liberals of just about everything, from operating a political slush fund to extorting votes in Quebec. In one of many such ruminations, Sage likened King to a "movie star losing her appeal to the public and afraid that one of her smarter and better looking rivals will put her nose out of joint. Mr. King is so fearful that he does anything that will please the crowd."

"Mr. Sage" was no piece of radio programming, but rather paid political advertising by the Conservatives. Needless to say, King and the Liberals were not amused. Upon winning the 1935 vote, the Liberals moved quickly to deal with the CRBC. By 1936, a new broadcast policy was in place.

The CRBC was gone, to be replaced by an organization known as the Canadian Broadcasting Corporation. While the CBC would receive some public funding, it would operate at arm's length of government, similar to the BBC in the United Kingdom. Like the CRBC, the CBC had two main tasks. The first was to operate a string of radio stations across the country and provide Canadian programming. The second was to regulate all radio in the country. For CKY and CKX in Manitoba, it was a fairly easy segue. The MTS stations simply moved from the CRBC to become CBC affiliates.

For the vast majority of Manitobans, jurisdictional disputes, broadcast policy and political machinations were the least of their concerns. The Depression struck the province with a vengeance. Annual per capita income declined from $466 in mid-1929 to $240 by 1932. Wheat prices that had averaged just over a dollar a bushel in the mid 1920s fell to 35 cents by 1932.

On top of the economic collapse came extreme weather. The decade saw record cold spells, drought and blistering heat.

Hordes of grasshoppers became an almost annual event in southern Manitoba. 1936 saw a record heat wave; on July 11, the temperature in Winnipeg hit 108 degrees Fahrenheit, or 42.2 degrees Celsius. Dust storms swept across the province, reducing visibility and carrying away rich farmland. With so much dust in the air, the province began to experience black rain. In describing one such storm, the *Free Press* noted that "the sun began to fade shortly after lunch, and as the darkness grew blacker, birds retreated to their nests and soothsayers boldly prophesied that the world was coming to an end."

In the midst of such chaos, radio emerged as a growth industry. For Manitobans, and indeed the vast majority of Canadians, the medium was the number one entertainment choice. It was cheap. While the cost of a modern day receiver was well above the means of most people, battery-run sets were still plentiful. Almost anyone with the proper batteries, a couple of spools and a coil of copper wire could cobble together an old-fashioned crystal set. "Farmers on relief could get their 35-cent dry cells on their relief allowances with a minimum of skullduggery," recalled James Gray in *The Winter Years*. There was also the issue of the two-dollar license fee, which many listeners simply chose to ignore. For those who did not own a receiver, the solution was to visit someone who did. Group radio listening became a social phenomenon.

American radio programming proved very popular. By now the US radio industry had developed into a sophisticated entertainment factory. Manitobans tuned into programs such as "Ma Perkins", the "Eddie Cantor Show", "Amos and Andy", "Bing Crosby", the "Jack Benny Show", and "Charlie McCarthy and Edgar Bergen." A number of these programs were aired on CKY, CJRC and, later, the Canadian Broadcasting Corporation.

Local Talent

Yet, local radio was far from devoid of Canadian content. Stations spent considerable time developing and promoting their own programming in what was becoming a more competitive marketplace. Programming hours were boosted. By early in the decade, the broadcast day started at 8 am, with sign-off at 11 or 11:30 at night. Some familiar voices also popped up on the local airwaves. Darby Coats returned to Winnipeg to become general manager of CKY, after jumping ship in 1928 to work for the Richardson radio station in Saskatchewan. Herb Roberts from CNRW had earlier left to work with CNR radio in Montreal. When the railway shut down its radio network, Roberts came back to Winnipeg as program director at CKY.

By far the most labour intensive programming was radio drama. All stations were involved to varying degrees, providing new opportunities for local actors, actresses and directors. The CJRC Players provided regular productions. One of CKY's most successful serials fell under the category of "blackface broadcasting." The program, known as Ebony and White, was no doubt influenced by the "Amos and Andy" comedy in which white actors portrayed themselves as under-privileged blacks. The weekly program featuring William (Bill) Seller (Mr. White) and Graham Rattray (Mr. Ebony) began in 1929 and ran for five years until Seller was appointed general manager of CKX radio.

Few prairie farmers can say the Depression changed their lives for the better, but that argument could be made about Esse Ljungh. Born in Sweden, Ljungh came to Canada seeking new opportunities. He landed a job as a farm labourer in Saskatchewan and later obtained his own farmland near Radville. When the Depression hit, Ljungh was wiped out and headed to Winnipeg to try to pick up the pieces. He returned to his theatrical roots having had some acting experience as a child and young man in Sweden. Ljungh worried his pronounced Swedish accent would not be suitable for the Canadian stage. He was wrong. He became involved with the Winnipeg Little Theatre Company and was soon acting and directing radio plays on both city radio stations. One of his early successes was a weekly program known as the "Youngbloods of Beaver Bend", which dramatized life on a western Canadian farm. Youngbloods was produced at CKY studios and ran on the CRBC network. Ljungh loved to work with sound and sound effects and developed new techniques in using sound in radio drama. The formation of the CBC opened new opportunities both in Winnipeg and ultimately Toronto. Ljunge would go on to be one of the most influential men in Canadian theatre, becoming National Supervisor of Drama for the Canadian Broadcasting Corporation.

Live music remained a programming staple. From country to crooners to classical, there was something for everyone. As with drama, radio was opening new opportunities for local musicians to promote themselves and, with any luck, perhaps earn a little money. One of CKY's early hires was a university student and piano player named Bert Shapiro. Better known by his stage name Bert Pearl, he would, within a decade, be the most popular radio musician in the country. At CJRC, Andy De Jarlis and his Red River Mates became a programming sensation. De Jarlis was

Andy De Jarlis. CKSB COLLECTION. LA SOCIETE HISTORIQUE DE SAINT BONIFACE.

the youngest of a 14-member family from Woodridge, Manitoba. He emerged as one of the top fiddlers in the nation, recording 33 albums, and was a fixture on local radio for more than 30 years. Soprano Gertrude Newton, the Pelman Richardson ensemble and Ukrainian songstress Jean Kuczer are but a few other examples of the array of local talent that was available to the listening audience.

The arrival of the CBC, coupled with increasing competition between CKY and CJRC, represented a significant boost for local actors and entertainers. While few artists got rich from working in radio, for the first time there was actually money available to pay for talent. "Probably no other effort has assisted employment, especially to musicians, more than radio," wrote Commissioner John Lowry, in the Manitoba Telephone System's 1939 annual report. "Total artists' payroll originating from our studios amounted to $127,202.80. In 1929 the comparative figure was less than $17,000. The advent of the Canadian Broadcasting Corporation, for which we are basic stations, assisted to a large extent in this increase."

When it came to music, local programmers soon discovered just how difficult it was to try to be all things to all people. For the most part, listener complaints centred on the seemingly endless conflict of old versus new. An emerging form of music known as jazz provoked a considerable outcry. "Ever since radio 'jazzed' up the air we have had nothing but hard times, so let us become sane again," wrote one disgruntled listener to CKY. Another was equally blunt. "My pet peeves are jazz, crooners, modern dance orchestras, and all such barbarians." The refrain would continue throughout the decades, as no one ever seemed quite satisfied with the music they heard on local radio.

A far greater programming controversy had nothing to do with music, but rather religion. As the CBC affiliate in Manitoba, CKY was under contract to the national broadcaster stipulating that certain hours were allocated for network programming. On Sundays, those hours were to begin at 7:30 pm. Almost since the beginning of radio, the Sunday evening time slot was given to local church broadcasts. When word leaked that the Sunday night service might be dumped, the reaction was fierce. "Please give us our Sunday church services," wrote one listener whose letter was typical of many received by CKY. "We don't live next door to a church, and in many country places they only have a service once or twice a month."

The debate became so heated the province's attorney general and the minister of telephones took the unusual step of issuing a public letter. In classic understatement, the politicians noted the topic had been the subject of "considerable discussion" and then announced that a compromise had been reached with the CBC whereby the Sunday evening church service would continue. The listeners had prevailed.

News and community affairs programming tended to mesh together. Radio stations had no newsrooms. Newscasts, which were aired two or three times a day, usually consisted of newspaper wire-copy.

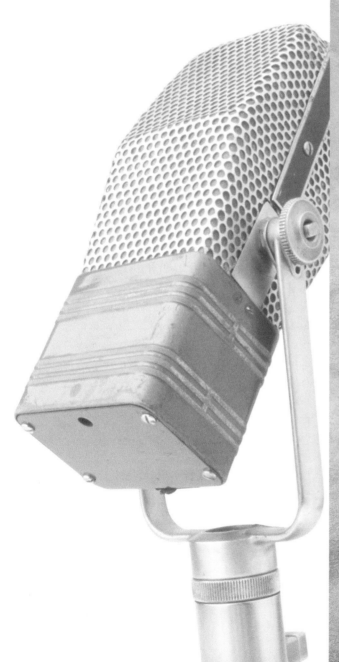

TOUGH AUDIENCE

Radio performers in the 1930s may have enjoyed celebrity status, but it also made them fair game for listener complaints. During the Depression, there was plenty of grouching about what was on the radio and how programming was delivered. To the credit of the Manitoba Telephone System, many of these complaints were made public in *Manitoba Calling*, a monthly publication about CKY and CKX radio. Below is a sampling of listener views:

"Announcers certainly need lessons in pronunciation. Some of them are terrible." *(Winnipeg)*

"Most of the singers who perform with the dance orchestras should be left overnight in a lethal chamber." *(Hartney, MB)*

"I wish you wouldn't run so many dramas with weeping women, frivolous daughters, wayward sons and so forth. Surely there is enough trouble in real life without filling our homes with stories of more misery." *(Winnipeg)*

"I feel like reaching for my shot gun every time I hear someone reading sloppy verses on the radio." *(Brandon)*.

"It's nice to know stations really are trying to improve the pronunciation of their announc-ers. While we all make mistakes, that does not excuse some of the blunders we hear, many of which must be attributable to simple ignorance, or, to be less harsh, shall we say inexperience. Announcers should be versatile, familiar with the best of good literature, and should have adequate cultural background." *(Winnipeg)*

Politicians were given ample, and, for the most part, equal time during the federal and provincial elections of 1935 and 1936. On election night, results were duly reported.

In the summer of 1938, local radio geared up for a story that had captured the world's imagination. Millionaire businessman and film producer, Howard Hughes, was attempting the first airplane flight around the world. One of the refuelling stops on the final leg of the 15,000-mile journey was to be Winnipeg. On July 11, the Hughes aircraft arrived in Edmonton on schedule. Winnipeggers began gathering at Stevenson's airfield as early as midnight that night, expecting to see history in the making. By 2 am, there was a huge crowd. At 4 am, city police moved in to ensure crowd control. Herb Roberts at CKY stood ready to provide live coverage of the historic event.

Overnight skies had become dark and cloudy. A "misty rain" reduced visibility. They waited, but there had been no contact with the Hughes plane for nearly eight hours. Then, just after 6:30, word came. Because of the weather, the aircraft had changed its route. It had arrived safely in Minneapolis. Herb Roberts and his colleagues had been up all night for the story that never happened.

Sports fans had plenty of reason to tune in. Led by CJRC and sportscasters Charlie O'Brien and Rusty Young, Winnipeggers could listen to everything from baseball to boat racing. Sports was a regular feature on Saturday afternoons with the station covering such events as Winnipeg Maroons baseball, the Kenora Regatta and, on at least one occasion, play-by-play golf. By 1935, O'Brien was describing the exploits of Fritz Hanson and other members of the Winnipeg rugby football club, forerunners of the Blue Bombers. These were among the earliest football broadcasts in the country. On September 21 of that year, O'Brien was at the microphone at Osborne stadium when the "Pegs", as they were best known, took on the defending champion Sarnia Imperials. Much to the delight of the 4,000 fans in attendance, the "Pegs" beat the Imperials. It was the first time since the Canadian Rugby Association was formed in 1892 that a team from the west had defeated an eastern rival. According to local newspapers, "the Pegs were the toast of the town," and football on the radio would become a Winnipeg tradition.

Sports were by no means limited to CJRC. Pity poor Herb Roberts at CKY. On a blistering hot July day in 1936, Roberts was perched atop the Winnipeg Tennis Clubhouse on Roslyn Road, providing coverage of the men's singles final. The weather office would later report it was the hottest day ever recorded in the province's history. Roberts faced the other extreme as well, providing play-by-play curling coverage on cold January nights from the Granite curling club. In addition to local sports, CKY was the World Series station, picking up play-by-play of the baseball classic from American networks. The 1935 Joe Louis-Max Baer world heavyweight boxing championship bout was also aired on CKY.

It was hockey on the radio that truly captured the imagination of listeners. Foster

Hewitt's hockey broadcasts from Maple Leaf Gardens in Toronto became a shared experience that helped define the Canadian identity. It was as if country and city shut down on Saturday nights to hear the hockey game. On farms, chores were done early. People who didn't own a radio would visit neighbors to hear the hockey game. There is one account of several neighbouring families packed into a tiny southern Manitoba farmhouse to hear "Foster." A fierce winter storm came up during the evening and the entire group spent the night in the home that barely had room for the family of five who lived in it. So intense was the hockey following that an otherwise gentle farm wife was heard to curse in front of the local minister when the opposing team scored on the Leafs.

Another story from the era further illustrates the magnitude of the hockey following and the power of radio. The hockey games were aired through the CRBC or later the CBC. In Manitoba, they were heard on CKY and CKX. One Saturday night the broadcast was interrupted. An injured man in a local hospital was in desperate need of blood. Within minutes, 300 calls poured in to CKY. The correct blood type was found and the patient made a full recovery. At no other time could the radio station have garnered such a huge audience of potential donors.

The size of radio audiences did not go unnoticed by those hoping to sell products. While there were restrictions on advertising (the price of a product could not be mentioned on the air), there was little doubt about the effectiveness of radio as a marketing tool. The following account in a 1937 edition of *Manitoba Calling* clearly demonstrates the power of the medium:

"Consider the recent demand for a knitting book, resulting from announcements by a well-known soap manufacturer. 8,500 letters have been received by CKY…That number will be significantly augmented by the time these lines are being read. Each letter has contained ten cents in stamps or coin of the realm, as well as a carton top."

By the mid '30s the battle was on between CKY and CJRC for advertising dollars. "During the year we have had very active commercial competition from the privately-owned station," wrote MTS Commissioner Lowry in the crown agency's 1936 annual report. CJRC had boosted its power to one thousand watts giving it better coverage throughout the city.

That same year, Dawson Richardson of CJRC established a small company known as All Canada Radio Sales. Its goal was to connect local radio with national advertisers who were, for the most part, located in eastern Canada. Richardson later merged his enterprise with a group from western Canada into what developed as one of the nation's first rep firms.

Radio North

Radio was also making its way north, and not just via freak sound waves from distant cities.

On November 14, 1937, CFAR radio went on the air in Flin Flon. At the time

Reverend Ray Horsefield.
FLIN FLON HERITAGE PROJECT

it was one of Canada's northern-most radio stations.

The station was the brainchild of one J.M. "Monty" Bridgman who operated a radio, auto and marine equipment shop. While in high school, Monty had become enamoured with the new medium of radio and dreamed of owning his own station. In many respects, Flin Flon was a stereotypical mining community. The discovery of copper and zinc had led the Hudson's Bay Mining and Smelting Company to establish a mine. Thousands flocked to the new community seeking work. By the early '30s, the town had an established business community which could even claim a flourishing "red light district." As early as 1934, Bridgman began promoting the idea of a radio station for Flin Flon. A company was formed under the name Arctic Radio Corporation. Investors included Bridgman's father George and businessman Joe Cousineau. The federal department of Marine and Fisheries approved a license for a new station, but there were still obstacles to be overcome. During those Depression

years, funds were in short supply, and the first 125-foot transmitter tower collapsed and had to be re-erected. Finally, early on a winter day in 1937, CFAR hit the airwaves, with studios in the rear of the Northern Cafe Building at 120 Main Street.

Over time, CFAR would become a vital communications tool, not only for Flin Flon, but much of Manitoba and Saskatchewan's northland. Early broadcasts were live and local. The music of "Welcome Morris and His Oldtimers" filled the airwaves from 1937 to 1944. Bert Wilson, who worked for the CNR, became a local celebrity calling barn dances. It was all but inevitable that the station would become the voice of the community's beloved Flin Flon Bombers hockey team. Whether it was forest fires or mining developments, CFAR did its best to keep listeners informed.

Like all radio stations of the era, CFAR served as an outlet for religious programming. Among those making use of the airwaves was the Reverend Ray Horsefield. The Anglican minister came up with the idea of putting together a short segment

of local information in the Cree language. Horsefield had taught himself to read and write Cree. He even had a special type-writer with Cree syllabic keys which he used to translate the Bible. His program was known as "Teepee Tidings". According to an account published by the Flin Flon Historical Society, within a month the favourable response encouraged CFAR, and Reverend Horsefield to begin a fifteen-minute program of "intimate bits of news, humorous anecdotes, news of fishing and trapping, messages from patients in hospitals, and answering questions about relatives all over the northland." "Teepee Tidings", and later "Teepee Chitchat", are believed to have been the first Cree lan-guage broadcasts in Canada.

CFAR can also take credit for launching the career of one of the province's better known politicians. Charles "Buck" Whitney was an announcer and served as general manager of the radio station for a decade. Whitney was a skilled orator and his radio presence gave him name recognition throughout the region. Whitney left CFAR

to run for political office and in 1959 was elected as the Conservative MLA for Flin Flon. He served in the Duff Roblin govern-ment as Minister of Natural Resources and Minister of Health.

For over a quarter century, CFAR was all but the exclusive voice of the North. Shortly after the war, the Canadian Armed Forces established a low-power station in Churchill to provide entertainment for military personnel. CHFC operated only eight hours a day. Eleven years later, the CBC took over operation of the station. On March 28, 1964, CHTM Thompson went on the air as a commercial radio station owned by a company known as Mystery Lake Broadcasting. In 1971, CHTM played a role in the formation of a new Aboriginal broadcasting organization called Native Communications Incorporated. Its goal was to provide information and entertainment to the native population, many living in remote and isolated communities. Initially, NCI broadcast programs for 90 minutes a day on CHTM. Later it would evolve into one of the largest Aboriginal broadcasting

networks in Canada. CFAR would become part of a three station northern network as Arctic Radio eventually assumed ownership of CHTM as well as CJAR in The Pas.

The King's Speech

For a brief moment in 1939, Winnipeg became the centre of the radio universe. The occasion was the royal visit to Canada by King George VI and Queen Elizabeth. For the newly-crowned monarch it was the first visit abroad. The CBC, with the full support of the King government, was determined to use the event to showcase the merits of public broadcasting. Close to one hundred CBC staff members were chosen to work the visit, providing cover-age from the second the royal couple set foot on Canadian soil until the day they left. A special school was set up to teach the broadcasters proper protocol. In the words of radio historian Sandy Stewart, "this re-markable troop spent six weeks in continu-ous travel, crossing seven thousand miles

to cover the tour. They produced ninety one broadcasts and in the process became heroes of the CBC."

While each stop had its own problems, the Winnipeg visit presented a unique broadcasting challenge. The King and Queen were scheduled to arrive on May 24, Victoria Day. To celebrate the holiday, the King was to use radio not just to address the nation, but the entire Commonwealth.

The city was in a frenzy over the royal visit. No less than 42 trains steamed into Winnipeg from all corners of the province and northwestern Ontario. Fifteen to 20 thousand people arrived from the United States. Eaton's, The Bay and all other downtown stores were draped in the Union Jack. A special grandstand was set up at Portage Avenue and Sherbrook Street so locals could get a better view of the royal parade. The cost of a seat was five dollars... an exorbitant sum for the 1930s.

Winnipeggers awoke May 24 to the sound of pouring rain. For a province ravaged by drought much of the decade, the downpour was an added blessing on this most exciting Victoria Day. Braving the weather, crowds began gathering on city streets in the early morning hours...over 150,000 according to some newspaper estimates. At 10:30, the Royal Train arrived at Union Station. CKY and CJRC had devoted their entire day to royal coverage.

Few, if any, in the throng that day could have realized just how nervous the King must have been as he and Queen Elizabeth made the short trip up Broadway to the Manitoba Legislature and Government House. Since early childhood, George had suffered from a severe stutter and had been undergoing intense training to overcome the disability. The prospect of a radio broadcast to his loyal subjects would not be something the King was looking forward to that wet Winnipeg day.

For weeks, CBC and CKY engineers had been setting up a makeshift studio at Government House, next door to the Legislature. Timing was crucial. The speech was to begin at 1 pm Winnipeg time so as to be heard at 8 pm in England. The King was to be in the room alone, with engineers and aids waiting just outside. The *Tribune* reported that furnishings in the room would "reflect relaxation." All broadcast lines, wiring and amplifiers were duplicated in an effort to prevent any technical failures.

As the King entered the tiny studio, he saw a single desk and a chair. On the desk were two small gold-plated microphones. Only one of these microphones would actually be used. The other was wired and ready to go, just in case the first did not function.

Sitting at the desk, the King began the broadcast as scheduled. Slowly, and at times hesitantly, King George VI spoke to the world from Winnipeg. According to the *Free Press*, the potential audience was 500 million people. In far flung nations, people huddled around radios to hear the speech. In England, the ailing Queen Mother was said to have followed the address closely while propped up in her bed. Thirteen-year-old Princess Elizabeth heard her father's speech in the sitting room in Buckingham Palace.

(George VI's Winnipeg broadcast took place a full three months prior to the radio address dramatized in the 2010 movie "The King's Speech.")

By 1939, radio in Manitoba had moved well beyond the experimental stage. Radio had become part of people's everyday lives. With two provincially-owned stations, two private stations and the CBC, the face of broadcasting had been established. There would be public and private radio, characterized by keen competition and, sometimes, conflict. While broadcasters clearly believed community service was an integral part of their business, advertising had become a fact of life that would ultimately shape the industry. Having survived the Depression, radio was about to face a new challenge...war.

CKY Victory sign located on Memorial Boulevard.
MANITOBA CALLING GARRY MOIR COLLECTION.

CHAPTER FOUR

Radio at War

From 1939 to 1945, radio was an instrument of war. It served as a vital source of information, and in some cases, disinformation. It was a propaganda tool, a morale booster and a fundraiser. Perhaps most important of all, it was a personal connection between the troops and the folks back home, thousands of miles away. "Canadian radio has pledged the support of its far flung facilities in the great task of accomplishing ultimate victory," trumpeted the local radio publication *Manitoba Calling*.

Midnight was fast approaching on September 3, 1939, but staffers at CKY, CJRC and Manitoba's two rural radio stations had no plans for heading home. Earlier in the day, all regular programming had been halted. Special news bulletins flashed over the airwaves as British Prime Minister Neville Chamberlain declared Britain was now in a state of war with Germany. With Canada a loyal member of the Commonwealth, listeners were well aware Canadians boys would soon be heading overseas.

By now CKY and CKX were firmly ensconced as CBC affiliates. The bulk of programming on both stations was originated by the CBC or picked up through the CBC from American networks. Although radio had been thriving for nearly 20 years, the CBC itself did virtually no news gathering. News events, like the Royal Tour, tended to be covered as specials with everyone at the radio station pitching in. The source for most daily news was wire service newspaper scripts. The outbreak of war changed everything. With Canadian troops on the front lines, there was a need and demand for news that had never existed before. In 1940, the CBC network established its own news service with four regional newsrooms including CKY Winnipeg. A reporter with the *Winnipeg Free Press* named William Metcalfe was lured away from the paper to head up the new Prairie division. He would later return to a long career as managing editor of the *Free Press*.

First CBC Winnipeg news director
William Metcalfe. WINNIPEG PRESS CLUB

Metcalfe, who was born in Portage la Prairie, was not one to pass up a party. It was New Year's Eve and the newly appointed CBC news director had celebrated well into the night. Somewhere between 4 and 5 am, he left a downtown restaurant, still decked out in coat, tails and homburg hat. He trudged across the snow at Portage and Main to the CKY studios in the Telephone Building on Main Street. Taking the elevator to the sixth floor, he sat down at his typewriter. Having been up all night, he hammered out the first prairie regional newscast aired by the CBC news service.

In addition to Metcalfe, that first newsroom consisted of three other members: newswriter Matt Smith along with copy boys Les Jackson and Bert Dentry. Mostly, the job consisted of reworking British United Press wire copy. Censorship rules were strict. In some cases the names or places of battles could not be used. There was to be no mention of sports, and under no circumstances was there to be any reference to gambling.

Once written, an announcer read the copy. The war presented numerous pronunciation challenges for on-air staff having to read unfamiliar names of foreign newsmakers or places. Most announcers had emerged from a music or entertainment background and were hired for their strong, resonant voices, not necessarily their knowledge of current affairs. The CBC, in its wisdom, offered this advice: "Consult the best available authorities and pronounce foreign names with such an approximation to the correct pronunciation that will leave the announcer free from the charge either of conscious superiority or careless ignorance." Sound sentiment, but of limited value when it came to reading names like Vyacheslav Molotov (Russian foreign minister) or Afsluitdijk (vital road link in Holland).

News on the radio became a "must listen." There are stories of people purposely not using their radios during the day to ensure their battery-powered receivers would hold up for the nightly newscast. A shortage of materials for radio batteries presented difficulties for the listeners throughout the conflict.

War Correspondents

Never in history had war news been presented with the kind of immediacy provided by radio. Early in the conflict, the CBC sent its men to the front. Reporter Bob Bowman and technician Art Holmes travelled to England with the first load of Canadian soldiers. Both were soon in the midst of battles, sending dispatches back to Canada, via the BBC. As the Nazis blitzed London, Holmes would take his specially-equipped van into city streets, recording the sounds of bombs falling. Other reporters followed, among them John Kannawin, a producer, announcer and administrator with CBC Winnipeg.

Kannawin's journey overseas was memorable. Unlike most other correspondents, he travelled across the ocean by air rather than ship. Transatlantic flight was, to say the least, in its infancy. Flying on a Liberator bomber, the trip from Dorval, Quebec to Scotland took 15 hours. Before leaving, Kannawin was required to sign a form absolving anyone of responsibility should something go wrong during the journey. According to fellow war correspondent A.E.Powley, Kannawin flew "lying on a mattress on the bomber's floor and wearing a flying suit, flying boots, helmet, mitts, oxygen mask, parachute pack and life jacket."

Flying did not end for Kannawin on arrival in the war zone. Based in London, he covered numerous battles, and during a visit to a base in Northern Ireland had the opportunity to fly on a military aircraft whose purpose was to ferret out and destroy German submarines in the north Atlantic. The tone and wording of his dispatch on that mission provides significant insight as to how war correspondents perceived their job.

"We had been instructed to wipe out enemy submarines and destroy them... the submarine hunt was already on. The Sutherland would dive on it, the front gunner would wipe out the deck gun crew, and depth charges would be shot out and down to it...I felt a strong and justifiable thrill of joy, for I was in a Canadian-manned aircraft guarding these precious sea lanes without whose control Britain could not survive."

Ironically, Winnipeg radio, initially at least, wanted nothing to do with another local lad who was to become one of the best-known war correspondents in the world. Stewart Macpherson had to travel to England to get his first crack at the world of broadcasting. "I couldn't even get an audition in Winnipeg," recalled Macpherson in an interview years later.

Perhaps not surprising. By his own admission, young Macpherson was a problem boy, filled with insolence and cheek. His father "tanned" him regularly; but even that had little impact on the truculent youth. "I hated school, wouldn't wash my neck, and had an outstanding apathy toward education," stated Macpherson in his memoirs. He dropped out of school, and a job as an undertaker's assistant turned out to be a dead end.

What young Stew did care about was sports. Almost to the point of obsession. He knew the players, the plays, the strategy and the statistics. While it was hard to find a sport Macpherson did not like, his passion was hockey. An obvious means of utilizing

such knowledge was to cover sports on a radio station, but Macpherson's reputation, along with his dismal education record, effectively blocked that possibility.

Seeing few prospects in Winnipeg, Macpherson took a leap of faith, deciding to travel to England. Passage to Great Britain was by way of a cattle boat. Macpherson could not find words to describe his miserable voyage across the Atlantic. "Even the cows complained," he recalled, "and all of us were seasick."

Following a brief stint of selling shoes, Stewart finally got his break when the BBC was looking for someone to broadcast the increasingly popular sport of ice hockey. Macpherson auditioned and, being the only applicant who knew anything about the game, got the job. He was an overnight sensation. British listeners had never heard anything quite like the staccato-styled play-by-play provided by this young Canadian. Because so many players were Canadian, the BBC put some matches on its short wave frequency. On New Year's Day, 1939, his family in Winnipeg gathered around the radio to hear "Stew" doing play-by-play from England. It seemed the "problem child" had turned a corner. No one could have predicted that within a year, Macpherson would be back in Winnipeg and out of a job.

With the onset of war, the BBC shifted its priorities. Most sports broadcasts were halted and Macpherson was again un-employed. Only a year and a half earlier, his longtime girlfriend had moved from Winnipeg to England and they were mar-ried. They now had a one-year-old child. Wife and child were sent home to Canada, but their ship was torpedoed in the Atlantic. Both survived, but Macpherson was not prepared to let them travel alone again. He reluctantly returned to Canada.

Much to his chagrin, Winnipeg radio was hardly more receptive than it had been before he left. In his memoirs there re-mained a tinge of bitterness. "My time in British broadcasting was spent for naught as far as my homeland was concerned," McPherson wrote. "Local radio stations had their staffs. They didn't want me." He did eventually land a sportscasting job with CJRC. After only a short time on the job, he was called into the office of gen-eral manager Tiny Elphicke. There was a telegram from the BBC. Macpherson was wanted back in England. This time as a war correspondent. There was no hesitation about leaving Winnipeg radio and heading to war-ravaged Europe. His replacement was an upstart broadcaster from Saskatoon named Jack Wells.

It was a true turning point. Over the next three years, Macpherson's war reports were heard around the world. With a knack of being at the right place at the right time, he reported on hundreds of stories for the BBC, many of which made their way back to Winnipeg via the CBC. Macpherson did it all. He flew in air raids, helped fill tanks with fuel during the Normandy invasion, rubbed shoulders with Patton and Montgomery and admitted to a good "piss-up" with Eisenhower. Yet his real stories didn't come from the offices of generals, but from the soldiers on the front lines. Like the men he covered, he witnessed the horrors

A MILITARY PERSPECTIVE

"In military terms, radio is a war machine, a war weapon. With it one plays upon the minds and hearts of men. It can be used to strengthen the moral fibre of a people at war, or it can be used to demoralize those far behind the fighting front. In a war where everything we have is at stake, as at the present moment...everything from prosperity to liberty to life...at such a time it is to be remembered that radio is essential in total warfare."

*Source: Major General L.R. La Fleche
Canada's Minister of National War Services
1942-1945*

"CKY'S LADY OPERATOR"

It was most unusual in a male-dominated industry: a woman working as a technical operator in the control room of a radio station. Because of a manpower shortage created by the war, women stepped into many positions which up until then had been considered a man's domain. There is no better example than that of Evelyn Whitebread, a young woman from St. Boniface who was called upon to handle all matters technical at CKY.

Whitebread was born in London, England and came to Canada as a child. She was a licensed amateur radio operator, which was in itself an unusual interest for a woman in that era. She spoke from her VE4 HZ in her St. Boniface home to "hams" in numerous countries, including Russia and Australia. When the war broke out, she devoted her talents to training men in Morse code, which still played a part in many military operations. Making her even more valuable was the fact she spoke French as well as English. In 1943, with many of CKY's technical operators off to war, Whitebread was a natural choice to fill a void that few others qualified for.

of war and had the skill to tell their stories. A.E. Powley relates what was perhaps Macpherson's closest call as Allied troops prepared to retake the French city of Caen.

"They (Macpherson and CBC correspondent Bill Fairburn) had been sitting on a low wall chatting with two British soldiers in slit trenches. Mortar bombs began falling around them and they dived to the ground. When the mortaring was over the two soldiers were dead."

This was an experience Macpherson never mentions in his memoirs.

Just how well-known was the young broadcaster from Winnipeg? In 1942, the British public voted him "Male Voice of the Year," edging out another well-known war hero...Winston Churchill.

While the correspondents provided vivid, albeit heavily-censored accounts of battles and other war developments, it was the voices of the soldiers themselves that brought the conflict home. Soldiers on leave in London would flock to the Beaver Club near Trafalgar Square. There they would line up for a chance to say a few words into a CBC microphone to the folks back home. The messages were usually no more than twenty to thirty seconds long. Nothing more than a "Hi Mom, Hi Dad," or perhaps a happy birthday or anniversary. Regardless, the connection was made. Soldiers would also be interviewed on a variety of programs, giving listeners on the home front another chance to hear their loved ones. The messaging, however, was by no means a one way street. Groups of women would visit CKY studios and record messages for their boys overseas. It was a roundabout process. The recording was done in Winnipeg. The discs were then shipped to Boston, where they were transmitted for rebroadcast on the BBC. The emotional impact of these voice encounters is impossible to quantify. Suffice to say these few words back and forth provided an intimacy unknown in any previous war.

Wartime programming

The war shaped radio in unexpected ways, not the least of which was a shorter broadcast day. In 1942, in a measure to conserve existing broadcasting equipment, radio stations in Canada curtailed their late evening schedules. Stations signed off the air a half hour earlier...in the case of CKY and CKX, sign-off came at 11:35 as opposed to midnight. The CBC evening national newscast was also pushed back an hour, the theory being that people would go to bed earlier, cutting back on consumption of materials needed for war.

Live music remained an integral part of local radio, ranging from the classical sophistication of Pehlman Richardson and his orchestra to the down home country charm of the Red River Barn dance, hosted by CKY morning man Tom Benson. Added to the mix was an array of military concerts, usually made up of local servicemen. At the request of the military, the weather forecast was not broadcast.

Dramas were produced for the expressed purpose of shaping public opinion. "Drama has a double part to play in wartime," declared the radio publication *Manitoba Calling*. "Stirring dramas with propagandist themes help to point the objectives for which we are fighting and the insurgencies of our war needs." Listeners tuned in to hear the daily trials and tribulations of "A Soldier's Wife" whose husband had gone off to war. It prided itself as the one program that tried to get people "not to buy" something. Sponsored by the Wartime Prices and Trade Board, which was responsible for rationing, the program was filled with messages about coupons, new rationing regulations and how to conserve products the country was running short on. Other popular CBC wartime dramas included "Carry on Canada" and "Newbridge", starring former Winnipegger Tommy Tweed. Newbridge depicted a rural Canadian township doing its part to help the cause.

Start

If Day

Thursday, February 19, 1942 stands out as one of the most unique days in the history of local radio programming. It was also one of the strangest days the province had ever witnessed. Tuning in shortly after 7 am, Winnipeggers were informed that "thousands of our troops are manning defence posts on the outskirts of the city. Street lights have been turned out in anticipation of an air raid and blackout regulations are being enforced." Scary stuff, and it was meant to be just that. Of course, Winnipeg wasn't really under attack. Radio stations were simply participating in "If Day." It was an "event" sanctioned by the Victory Loan Committee, an arm of the federal government, to boost the sale of victory bonds to fund the war. Organizers went to extreme lengths to demonstrate what it would be like, should the Nazis ever occupy the city and province. People were hired as German soldiers who would storm the city. Various regiments would try to fight back, with both sides firing blanks to make the

encounter seem more realistic. War planes buzzed low over Winnipeg. Air raid sirens sounded, bridges were closed, churches boarded up, books burned at the local library. German soldiers with Bren guns patrolled Portage Avenue.

The Premier and the Mayor were "arrested" and held captive at Lower Fort Garry. By nightfall, the entire province was under Nazi control. Radio stations broadcast all the goings on, although there were announcements throughout the day that this was indeed a mock invasion. Of particular concern for organizers was the possibility that Americans, hearing the broadcast, might panic. US border towns were warned in advance. Students went to school that day, but after the invasion, classes ended so that they could listen to a radio drama entitled ``Swastika Over Canada." Other radio programming highlights that day included German martial music and excerpts of speeches by Herr Hitler himself. Broadcaster and actor George Waight, best-known as the CKY Santa Claus, got directly into the act. He played the role of

a German military leader in hot pursuit of Winnipeg's police chief who had somehow "eluded" capture. In retrospect, the entire charade could be viewed as nothing more than a propaganda/fundraising exercise in which radio was a willing participant.

Hard on the heels of` "If Day" came "Freedom to Play Night." The event, held at the Amphitheatre on Osborne featured a who's who of the local sports crowd and was broadcast in its entirety on CJRC. The purpose once again was to sell Victory Bonds. Five thousand people turned out to hear speakers, watch figure skaters and a junior hockey game. The main attraction, however, was Toronto hockey broadcaster Foster Hewitt, who urged those on hand not to hold back when it came to investing in the war. "They (Canadian troops) should be liberally supported with the best and most guns, ammunition, explosives, planes and ships that Canada can make or buy. If the sportsmen of Winnipeg, if the people of Canada will shoot the dollars through the medium of the second Victory Bond loan, Canadian soldiers will do the scoring."

Radio listeners as well as those at the rink were then treated to hearing Foster doing play-by-play of the third period of the Winnipeg Rangers and Monarchs hockey match.

Hewitt's NHL hockey broadcasts were more popular than ever, with the games being transmitted and rebroadcast to Canadian troops in Europe. At the same time, however, Foster's popularity was being challenged by a former Winnipegger named Bert Pearl, whose daily radio show offered its own brand of escapism. Pearl and his troop, known as the Happy Gang, captured the imagination of Canadians. With its trademark opening of "Knock, Knock—Who's There—It's the Happy Gang," the program offered a mix of feel-good music and lighthearted banter that allowed listeners to forget about the war for at least a few minutes each day. By 1950, the show was garnering an audience of over two million people.

The irony was that Pearl, a brilliant musician and band leader, was anything but happy. The man who had cut his teeth

Happy Gang promotional book.
GARRY MOIR COLLECTION

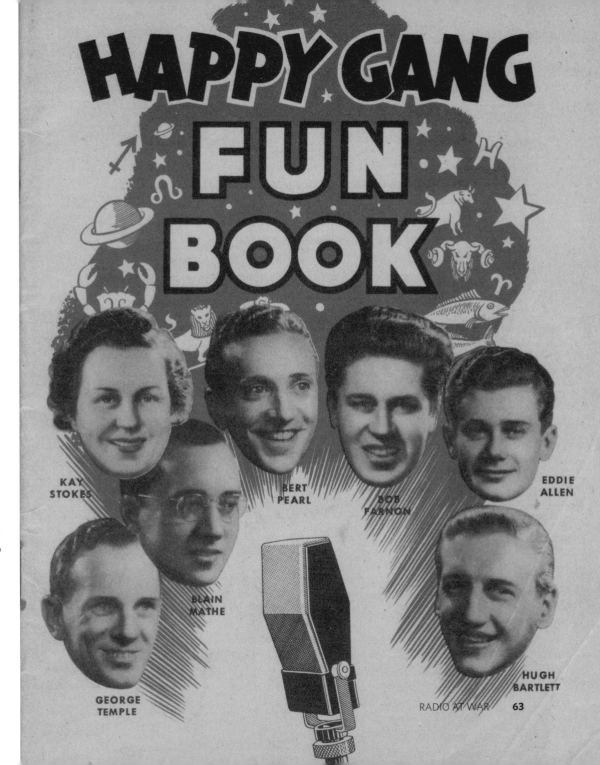

Good Deeds

Radio's audience was young, and thanks to programs like the Eaton's Good Deed Club, getting younger all the time. The Club, started in 1939, was heard on CKY radio Saturday mornings. The basic premise was simple. Young members signing up for the club were expected to do good deeds. Children aged five to 15 could enrol. Each week, "good deeds" were submitted and evaluated by a panel of judges. The winner of the good deed of the week received a gold watch from Eaton's, and sometimes a War Savings Bond.

The second component of the radio program was to promote young talent. Every Tuesday, club members wanting to appear on the show would audition. If successful, they would then provide the entertainment for radio listeners on Saturday morning. Over the course of the program there were the usual piano players, violinists and vocalists. There was also yodelling, drumming, and on at least one occasion, a magician. (Exactly how the youth performed his tricks

in Winnipeg radio in the 1920s would eventually suffer a nervous breakdown. He was high-strung, demanding and exercised almost total control over every aspect of the program. "Pearl has wounded the feelings of almost every employee he has ever had," wrote June Callwood in an often cited article in *Maclean's* magazine. "With one or two exceptions, the Gang feels nothing warmer than respect for the boss." Broadcaster and radio historian Sandy Stewart offered a somewhat softer interpretation. "Bert worked continuously at improving his show. He employed the best talent he could find, paid them well, and expected them to earn their money."

on radio is not certain.) A boys' choir and a girls' choir were developed which, in addition to singing on the radio, participated in music festivals around the city.

On Saturday mornings, the third floor halls of the CKY building on Main Street were jammed with youngsters who had come for the show. At 10:30, the mellifluous tones of chief announcer Wilf Davidson, and later Bob Wilson, would ripple over the air waves. "The Good Deed Club is on the air!" That was the cue for the boys' and girls' choirs to sing the standard opening many could still recite decades later:

"Do a good deed every day.
Obey the Golden rule.
Never say an angry word
or be unkind or cruel.
Scatter seeds of happiness
at home, at play, at school.
You'll find there's sunshine everywhere,
Obey the golden rule."

In its first three years, the Club attracted more than 18,000 members. Five years later that number had swelled to 30,000. With the exception of the Saturday night hockey broadcast, the Good Deed Club was consistently the most popular weekend radio program. The show provided the first broadcasting exposure for many future entertainers...among them band leader and musician Ted Komar, Garry Peterson, drummer for the Guess Who, Dan Wood, senior drama producer for the CBC, and noted Canadian pianist Gary Gross. The public relations value and revenue generated for Eaton's department store was incalculable.

One of local radio's greatest contributions to the war effort also created one of the industry's greatest problems. As in every other economic sector, broadcasters signed up to fight, leaving stations with a shortage of workers. Jack Holmes, Ron Deacon, C.M. "Dibbs" Woods, Tom Benson, Calvin Pepper, Wilf Davidson and D.R.P. Coats are but a few of the familiar broadcasting names that joined the forces. New voices popped up on the radio scene, such as Norm Micklewright, Earl Cameron and Dudley Patterson, all of whom would go on to distinguished broadcasting careers. Cameron for a time read the National News on CBC television.

Women assumed many roles which until then had been considered a man's domain. Edith Whitebread became the first female control room operator at CKY, while in Brandon, Peggy Fyfe served as a morning show announcer, alternating with Russ Carrier. Actress Beth Lockerbie was a regular voice on CKY in numerous capacities.

POW

Few broadcasters paid a higher price for their war service than CKY's Brian Hodgkinson. His story also illustrates just how important radio had become, even to those behind enemy lines.

The date was October 27, 1941. Most Manitobans were still asleep as an RCAF Spitfire was speeding across the English Channel. At the controls was young Hodgkinson, who a few months earlier had

start
↓

been reading the news and handling other announcer duties at CKY.

Brian Hodgkinson was born and raised in St. James. His father was Irish, his mother English. The baby-faced Hodgkinson had been blessed with a rich bass voice to go with his six-foot-six-inch frame. Like many of his generation, the Depression took its toll. He rode the rails in search of work, was caught and even spent a night in jail. He had an interest in theatre and was hired by CKY in the late 1930s, where he quickly became one of the station's most popular voices. With the outbreak of war, he was one of the first to sign up to fight.

On that fateful October day, the Spitfire was intercepted by enemy aircraft… the plane strafed by a barrage of bullets. Hodgkinson found himself spiralling downward in an airplane out of control. He managed to jettison himself from the aircraft and yank the ripcord of his parachute. When he landed near Calais, France, he was burned, bleeding, severely injured and surrounded by German soldiers. For

the remainder of the conflict, Hodgkinson would be a Prisoner of War.

Over the next four years, Hodgkinson faced experiences he could never have imagined. In his memoirs, he described a train trip through Germany as POWs were moved from one camp to another. The boxcar, Hodgkinson recalled," was at most about "half the size of Canadian or American rolling stock. Even so the goons had stuffed 55 of us into this black hole. So crowded were we that we could neither lie down or straighten our legs from sitting positions. We had less than two square feet of space for each man." The only ventilation was a two-by-two-foot window at the end of the car about six or seven feet from the floor. There were no washrooms.

For three long days, the soldiers survived the moving prison, basic human dignity all but forgotten. On arriving at their destination, they were herded out, mired in their own excrement. So bad was the smell that German guards covered their faces to avoid the stench.

It was at a prison camp known as Stalag 383 that Hodgkinson got back to his radio roots…sort of.

Among his POW mates was an Englishman described as an electronics fanatic. In civilian life, he was the chief engineer for a major manufacturer of wireless radio receivers. The Englishman convinced his colleagues that using scraps of copper wire, batteries and other materials found around the compound he could build a radio that would pick up the BBC to keep them up to date on the latest war developments.

The only thing they didn't have was a handful of glass radio tubes necessary to make the contraption work. This is where Hodgkinson came in. He and some other prisoners had developed a good relationship with certain German guards and had been allowed out of the POW camp on work excursions such as clearing brush or gathering wood. During these outside ventures, contact had been made with the German underground and arrangements were made to have the tubes dropped in an abandoned chicken coop near the camp. The only hurdle left was how to get the tubes past security on the way back into the compound.

One of the more enterprising POWs concocted a scheme that only desperate men would even consider, much less agree to: put the peanut-sized tubes in a place the guards would never look. In his memoirs Hodgkinson quotes the young genius.

"A little margarine to ease entry, and nine of our blokes will come back into camp with glass assholes."

On the appointed day, the tubes were collected and secured in their secret passageways. A flatus-free trip through security and the prisoners had all they required to make a radio. The clandestine operation was a complete success. The wireless receiver was assembled and worked like a charm. No wartime radio was more appreciated.

D-Day

Early one morning in July, 1944, a CKY executive was roused from his bed. A police car was on the way to his home. Two other CKY employees were also picked up as the cruiser headed through the empty city streets to the Manitoba Telephone Building. By the time they arrived, the third floor was already buzzing with activity. The British United Press news wire was pounding out dispatch after dispatch. As Winnipeggers turned on their radios to start a new day, they heard news that had been speculated about for months. Allied troops had landed in northern France. The liberation of Europe was underway.

The D-Day broadcast served as a dress rehearsal for what was to happen ten months later. Hitler's troops were in disarray, and it had become obvious it was only a matter of time before Germany capitulated. Radio stations in Winnipeg, and across the country, had been preparing for months for the big day. On May 1, 1945, word came that something was about to happen. Local radio went on the air in the wee hours of the morning. CKY took to the airwaves at 4 am on Tuesday morning. Speculation was rampant, but developments were slow. On May 7, just as many Winnipeggers were heading to work, the blast of an air raid siren came from the *Free Press* building. Broadcasters rushed to their microphones with a terse news bulletin. Germany had finally surrendered.

From that moment, all regular programming was abandoned. Commercials did not run. The party was underway. Although the weather was cold, windy and generally miserable, Winnipeggers took to the streets. According to one newspaper account, strangers hugged, cheered, laughed and cried together. Thousands gathered at Portage and Main. Eaton's and the Bay were draped in flags, while parades and church services were organized. As part of its advance preparation, CKY had developed a "mobile unit"... a vehicle that could travel from place to place and broadcast live on location. Technical facilities had also been set up at the *Tribune* so that editors could offer commentaries and analysis. Churchill's message was broadcast live, as were the words of King George VI. It was a gargantuan effort on the part of local radio. When CKY radio signed off at 11:35 Tuesday evening, it had been on the air 165 consecutive hours, a feat no station in Manitoba had ever accomplished.

With the surrender of Japan a month later, the war was over. The world would never be the same. Nor would the business of radio. So much had changed in just five years. Some of it had nothing to do with the war. CKY had a new frequency—990 on the dial. CKX had new studios officially opened in 1941. Winnipeg's only private radio station had a new owner. Following the sudden death of James Richardson in 1939, CJRC was sold to the powerful Sifton family, which already had an influential media empire, owning several newspapers across the Prairies, including the *Winnipeg Free Press*. At the request of the Richardson family, the call letters of the station were changed to CKRC located at 630 on the AM dial. The Siftons also moved the CKRC studios from the Royal Alex Hotel to a state of the art facility in the *Free Press* building on Carlton Street.

Broadcast technology had advanced. Wire recorders were now being utilized,

mobile units could provide reliable on the spot coverage and long distance broadcasting was so common it was almost taken for granted. Radio was now the go-to medium for the latest news. The celebrity journalist was in vogue. Careers had been launched, altered and, in some cases, ended. More women were involved in the industry.

Throughout the war, American programming continued to be extremely popular in Canada, with standards like Fibber McGee and Molly, Jack Benny and the Lux Radio Theatre among the favourites of local listeners. Between CKY, CKX and CKRC, Manitobans had access to all popular American shows. Canadian radio was also growing. By the end of the war, more Canadian programming was available than ever before.

After years of shortages and rationing, there was a pent-up demand for goods and services, both old and new. Radio had more than demonstrated its power to sway opinion and move products. Radio in Manitoba was set to expand.

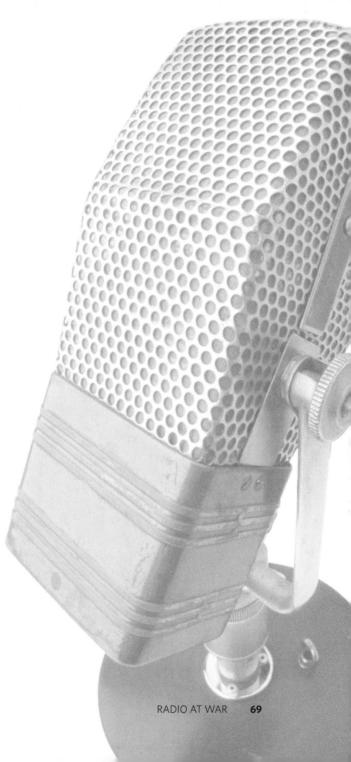

CHAPTER FIVE

The Original Six

Rural electrification played no small part in the growth of radio in Manitoba. As the war drew to a close, the Manitoba Power Commission embarked on an ambitious plan to bring electricity to 50,000 farm homes over the next decade. Sixty percent of the province's population lived outside Winnipeg and, with no electrical service, was dependent on cumbersome, and sometimes temperamental, battery-operated receivers to hear their favourite programs.

As electricity arrived, radio sales took off. A survey in the early 1950s asked rural residents which electrical appliance they used most. The radio turned out to be the easy winner, finishing well ahead of even the washing machine and toaster. More radios meant more listeners, and more listeners meant greater potential for advertisers selling products in an expanding post-war economy.

Radio was less than a quarter century old, but already the medium had a well-established business model based on advertising and sponsorships. Its power to sell products was undeniable. The name General Motors became synonymous with Foster Hewitt's hockey broadcasts. Colgate only advertised on the Happy Gang program. A campaign promoting the Colgate Palmolive soap

flakes had to be pulled when the manufacturer couldn't keep up with demand. Between 1935 and 1945, CKY and CKX saw revenues increase from $109,000 to over $352,000. "There is no letup in the amount of business being offered by advertisers desiring to use the medium of radio," wrote Commissioner John Lowry, in the 1944 annual report of the Manitoba Telephone System. A year later, he added that "applications for advertising are increasing and exceed by a considerable margin the amount of space apportioned for commercial broadcasts."

All this despite stringent regulations governing radio advertising. No prices could be mentioned, commercials were not permitted in the evening, and spot

Opposite: CJOB founder John Oliver Blick, with Rory MacLennan (pipe) and Chuck Potter Sales Manager at Hudson's Bay Company. MACLENNAN FAMILY

advertising could only take up five percent of the broadcast day. As the potential for big payoffs grew, private broadcasters lobbied hard for change. They were particularly irked by the fact that the CBC had been granted the power to regulate and license radio, while at the same time competing with private broadcasters for advertising dollars.

It was against this backdrop that a 30-year-old entrepreneur from Alberta rode into Winnipeg, with visions of launching a new radio station. John Oliver Blick was flamboyant, ambitious and, most importantly, a risk taker. Born in Edmonton of Scottish descent, Blick started out as a school teacher at $55 a month. His broadcasting career began when he went to work in the continuity department at radio station CJCA Edmonton, writing commercials. "I didn't even know what continuity meant," recalled Blick in an interview years later. While his time at CJCA was brief, he obviously learned one important lesson: there was more money to be made owning a radio station than working in one.

The war allowed Blick to follow another of his passions, which was flying. He joined the air force and became a flight instructor at Pearce, Alberta. According to lore, perpetuated by Blick himself, the idea for a radio station was "formulated in the mind of a youthful Royal Canadian Air Force pilot as he roamed the skies during World War II." Another story had Blick and his wife arriving in Winnipeg after the war "without a penny to their name."

While hardly reduced to penury, Jack Blick did not have the means to start a radio station. What he did have was a vision and an influential Winnipeg friend whom he had met during his time in the RCAF. That friend was Edmond Boyd Osler, whose late father was a charter member of Winnipeg's business elite. The mortgage and investment firm of Osler, Hammond and Nanton had played a formidable role in developing Winnipeg at the turn of the century. Edmond Boyd, better known as E.B., not only had money, but also knew others with access to capital. The consummate salesman, Blick was able to convince a group

of local investors of the merits of a new radio station. Not that it would have been a terribly hard sell. Winnipeg was growing and was the only major city in Canada with only one private radio station, that being CKRC, owned by the Sifton family. Both CKY and CKRC were affiliates of the CBC, so neither station could claim to be providing exclusive local programming. Blick saw this as his niche. The original board of directors included Osler, Kenneth Powell (former president of the Winnipeg Grain Exchange), grain dealer Clyde Eggleston, lawyer James Coyne (who would later be appointed a Justice of the Manitoba Court of Appeal), and Jack Perrin senior, a gold mining executive who would help bring professional hockey to Winnipeg.

The CBC, which licensed radio stations, approved the new entry into the Winnipeg marketplace. On March 11, 1946, at 6 pm, CJOB radio went on the air at 1340 on the dial, with 250 watts of power. Studios were located on the tenth floor of the Lindsay Building on Notre Dame, near Portage Avenue. Most assumed the JOB in the station's call letters stood for John Oliver Blick. Blick maintained the key word was "job." His vision was to start a business that would provide jobs for service people who had returned from the war. Indeed, every one of the original 26 employees had been in the armed services. "I wanted the station to be always on the job working for Winnipeg," said Blick, in an interview a number of years after the station opened. "Working for Winnipeg" would become CJOB's motto.

Gaining a toehold in the local market was a gargantuan challenge facing the new kid on the block. Having been on the air two decades, CKY and CKRC were firmly established with a loyal listenership. Combined, the two stations carried all of the popular network and syndicated programming. The Saturday night NHL hockey broadcasts were heard on CKY, as was perennial favourite Ma Perkins and the ever popular Happy Gang. A farm drama known as "The Jacksons" was also pulling a big audience over the noon hour. The Siftons had invested heavily in CKRC,

which featured highly-rated US programs such as Superman, the Lone Ranger, Charlie McCarthy and Edgar Bergen, Bing Crosby, Romance Theatre and the Friday night fights. CKY and CKRC had become tourist attractions as well, with people flocking daily to their studios to watch live local programming. CKRC on Carlton Street had become an edifice for all to see. Former employee Patrick McDougal offered this description of the radio station: "Its studios and offices in the *Winnipeg Free Press* building were truly breathtaking, enough to excuse the station for setting out its call letters in blue ribbon on stationery and advertising.

Visitors reached CKRC through a separate neon-lit entrance at the head of a spiral staircase that led from the building's impressive lobby to the floor above. There, under a neon sign that spelled out the station's call letters, another staircase—this one carpeted—waited just beyond chromed double doors. Climbing this second staircase got you at last to the station's foyer where a double-paned window took up most

of one wall. At noon hour, a crowd often gathered there to watch a popular duo perform on twin grand pianos in the studio beyond the glass. There were two other grand pianos on the premises, and one of them could be found on the stage of a full-fledged theatre that could accommodate some fifty people in padded seats. Employees of rival stations in Winnipeg displayed their jealousy by calling CKRC's announcers "movie stars" because they were so often "put on display, dressed to the nines."

Staff at CJOB must have wondered what they were up against, but Blick was more than ready to do battle. In an initial attempt to carve out a niche, CJOB chose not to run any commercials during the first week on the air. Instead, the station's studios were opened to charities, service clubs and veterans' groups to promote themselves. At a celebratory dinner marking the station's opening, director James Coyne pledged CJOB would provide "the best possible service and programmes, (and) refrain from spoiling programmes by inopportune commercial announcements." Within a year,

CJOB would join other private broadcasters demanding the federal government permit more time for commercials on the radio.

Innovation was a key component of the CJOB business strategy as the station would soon lay claim to a number of broadcasting firsts. It was the first radio station in Winnipeg to be on the air 24 hours a day. As it turned out, there were quite a number of night owls ready to listen. Staff announcer Phil Isley, one of the first to pull the graveyard shift, recalls spending "two hours" opening mail prior to each shift.

Musically, CJOB claimed a library of 9,000 recordings, featuring "all the popular artists of stage, screen, and radio fame." The station hired entertainer Monte Greene as staff pianist. Among the original programs was Club 1340, featuring the hit music of the day. The program would eventually attract such notables as Frankie Lane and Nat King Cole to the CJOB studios. Other programs included Classical Gems, Meet the Dance Bands, Friendly Tavern and, on Saturday nights, the "Herbie Brittain Orchestra." One of the first hires at CJOB was a 23-year-old announcer named George McCloy. Over the years he would serve many functions, including host of a country program where he was known as "Hank" McCloy. Later he served up homemaking advice with co-host Hedi Lewis. What his soothing voice is best remembered for, however, is a program for "shut-ins"... listeners who were confined to their homes for health reasons. In 1946, this was no insignificant audience. Many veterans were still confined to hospitals or other care facilities because of war injuries. Manitoba was in the middle of an ongoing polio epidemic, and there was the usual aging population. "The Shut-Ins" show became a Winnipeg institution which would evolve into a fundraising charity. The program would run for 40 years, ending when McCloy retired in 1987.

The first promotions manager at CJOB was Roderick M. "Rory" MacLennan. He was hired just days before the new station went on the air at a salary of $150 a month. Although he had no radio experience, his resume included two elements Blick liked. He was fresh out of the Air Force, and he was Scottish. His wartime experience included a stint piloting PBY Flying Boats in Florida...a highly secret mission where not even his wife was allowed to contact him. MacLennan also spent time in St. Ives, Cornwall, as part of the "Channel Watch", participated in the invasion of Normandy and flew the "Murmansk Route" protecting supply ships making their way to Russia.

MacLennan played an integral role in developing the "Working for Winnipeg" slogan that became synonymous with CJOB. His seemingly innate understanding of value of promotions and community service helped establish CJOB as the station that was "closer to the community." In 1951, CJOB received the John J. Gillen award for "outstanding community service in the interest of charity." Among its activities, the station raised more than a quarter of a million dollars for the Sanitarium Board of Manitoba to fight tuberculosis. It was also under MacLennan's watch that CJOB reached out to the First Presbyterian Church. The Reverend

Bruce Miles was commissioned to provide a daily sixty second inspirational message. "A Moment of Meditation" ran for more than three decades.

Rory MacLennan also discovered very quickly how rough and tumble the world of private broadcasting could be. After three years on the job, he was called into Blick's office and fired without warning. "I was told to get out and find out what other people are thinking," he recalled in an interview years later. Six years passed before Blick concluded he had made a mistake and re-hired his former promotions man as sales manager. A committed pipe smoker, MacLennan became an avuncular figure around CJOB. He would go on to become general manager and president of CJOB, guiding the station through its most successful years and making it one of the most profitable radio stations in North America.

It was in the area of news and information that CJOB was a true innovator. CJOB was the first station to offer news "on the hour every hour"...again a dramatic break from the four or five newscasts provided at

HUMBLE SERVANT—RADIO GIANT

During the height of World War II, British Prime Minister Winston Churchill slipped quietly into Gander, Newfoundland. Home of one of the Allies most strategic air bases, Gander was teaming with military personnel. While the exact purpose of Churchill's visit has never been clear, suffice it to say it was not a pleasure trip. The Prime Minister did, however, have a little relaxing time. Taken to the officer's mess, he was served Johnny Walker whiskey by a young Canadian airman doubling that day as bartender. The two men struck up a brief conversation. The Prime Minister may well have been impressed at the ease with which the young man handled himself. When Churchill finished his drink, the barman picked up the glass, gave it a quick wipe and slipped it into his pocket. It would become a family heirloom.

The name of the bartender was Roderick M. "Rory" MacLennan. Churchill had rubbed shoulders with a future broadcasting giant. In years to come, MacLennan would become an influential force in Canadian radio as general manager of CJOB Winnipeg, one of the most successful radio stations in North America.

other outlets. Engineers outfitted a mobile news cruiser, allowing live reports from traffic accidents, fires and other breaking news. This "beat of the street" approach fit perfectly with the "Working for Winnipeg" brand. CJOB also became the first station to provide live broadcasts of city council meetings.

A major challenge occurred on October 22, 1947. Winnipeggers went to the polls that day in a civic election and CJOB management was determined the station would be first with results. The station took out a large advertisement in the daily newspapers proclaiming "Special Broadcast Tonight— Men and Microphones move to the tabulation room in city hall for Flash Election Results." For Chief Engineer Reg Drurie and newscasters Allan Bready and Dudley Patterson, this was no small undertaking. No station had tackled this before. As the results were posted, announcers read them live over the air. While there were no doubt the usual glitches that are part of doing live election coverage, the concept worked. Within two years, CJOB had established

itself as the "go-to" station for breaking news, and, in so doing, carved a base that would ensure it lasting success.

Jack Blick himself worked tirelessly to ensure his station's success. Unlike many owners, he was the face of CJOB. Browsing through the social pages of the daily newspapers in the 1940s and '50s, it seems Blick was everywhere...whether it was a Chamber of Commerce meeting, a Burns supper or a women's meeting. He was a member of numerous veterans' groups, service clubs and business organizations. In many ways, this perfectly suited Blick's personality. He was gregarious and comfortable in a social setting. He was known as a "partier," recalled CJOB veteran Bill Stewart. A penchant for flashy cars was another Blick characteristic. As he became more affluent, Jack would cruise the city on summer nights in a 1953 Cadillac Eldorado Special Sport convertible.

The combination of fast cars and social butterfly didn't always serve Blick well. In early 1948, he was fined $50 and had his licence suspended for one month for reckless driving. He was clocked at 70 miles an

hour on a city street. Blick's defense was that he owned a 1947 Buick with safety tires. In passing sentence, the judge noted this was not his first offence. The ultimate irony came only a short time later when Blick was named President of the Manitoba Highway Safety Council. (In 1958, Blick was hospitalized after cracking up his car on a clear June afternoon. According to police reports he was driving on Donald Street between York and Broadway when his car went out of control and hit a hydro pole.)

In January 1947, CJOB pulled a harebrained publicity stunt that could well have served as inspiration for future television sitcom WKRP. "Smile, Darn Yah, Smile" was the name of the CJOB morning show, and for considerable time, host Chuck Cook had been talking about giving away $500. At no time, however, did he disclose exactly how this would be done. Just after 8 am on a Friday morning, pedestrians trudging to work on Notre Dame Avenue looked up to an amazing site. Money was floating downward from the CJOB studio window on the tenth floor of the Lindsay building.

Cook was on the air, hyping the promotion with a promise of more cash to come. Pandemonium is the only word to describe what happened next at Portage and Notre Dame. "Cars, bikes and buses brought hundreds of hungry souls to the street beneath the studio," reported the *Tribune*. As the cash drifted downward in a light wind, "people on the street fought for it. They ignored cars and buses as they ran blindly" (onto the street). There was a massive traffic jam, lasting almost an hour. Trolley buses could not get through and police were called to quell the crowd. What did people risk their lives for? As it turned out, "monopoly money." The cash floating in the wind was phoney. In one foul swoop, CJOB had managed to anger just about everybody. Initially, the station's switchboard had been overloaded with calls from listeners upset because they had not been given advance notice of the cash giveaway. Those who did make it to Notre Dame were disgruntled as they discovered the bills were fake. Transit was incensed because the traffic tie-up had disrupted bus schedules. Police had been faced with a potential riot. There is no indication CJOB was ever charged, but John Oliver Blick was obviously feeling the heat. A week later he donated a $500 cheque to the University of Manitoba, emphasizing that, this time, the money was "real." Morning man Chuck Cook eventually moved on to become a Member of Parliament from British Columbia. For better or for worse, CJOB had set itself apart from other radio stations in the city.

A broadcasting visionary, Jack Blick was not one to dwell on past mistakes or promotions gone wrong. In 1948, he was given a licence to set up CJOB FM, the first FM radio station in western Canada. "You get the feeling the orchestra is right in your living room when you receive FM transmission," enthused Blick. Yet in 1948, the move to FM was hardly conventional wisdom among the broadcasting elite. FM had only arrived in Canada a year earlier with experimental operations run by the CBC. "FM radio will not become common in western Canada for some time," predicted E. Kelsey, a well-known radio engineering consultant from Montreal. Speaking at a convention in Winnipeg shortly before CJOB FM went on the air, Kelsey observed that "of the CBC FM stations now operating in Montreal and Toronto, I doubt if either has more than 50 listeners. Private stations won't find enough profit to make it worth their while." But the future would tell a very different story, and the future was what Blick was all about. By the end of the decade he was already dabbling in the next major development in broadcasting—television. Although CJOB's glory years were still ahead, the new kid was already a force to be reckoned with in the world of Winnipeg radio.

Radio Ouest Française

Only three months after the arrival of CJOB, another "private" radio station hit the Winnipeg airwaves...this one very different than anything the city had seen before. The new station programmed in French and was conceived, not in Winnipeg, but far to the west.

Prud'homme, Saskatchewan seems an unlikely place to plant the seed for a new radio station in Manitoba. The French-speaking farm community northeast of Saskatoon had no connection to the broadcast industry and was best known for its numerous name changes. Yet in 1941, radio was very much on the mind of a local clergyman. Father Maurice Baudouin, along with other francophone leaders across the West, had been worried for some time about the impact of the medium on French language and culture. Radio, after all, was predominantly English, run mostly by British Protestants. On a warm August day, Baudouin invited six Catholic leaders to his home to discuss these concerns.

Out of that meeting came a new organization known as Radio Ouest Française (French West Radio). Its goal was to develop private French language radio on the Prairies.

The francophone leaders believed they could make a strong case that French was woefully under-represented on the airwaves. One of the earliest attempts at

French programming was heard on CJRW Winnipeg in 1929. A local Metis named Maurice Goulet hosted a series of concerts on a program known as the "French Heure." It ran for less than a year before being cancelled by the Richardson station. Promoters and participants were deeply disillusioned. The station claimed the audience was too small, but young Goulet was unconvinced. He saw "influence jaune la dessous," or a yellow influence underlying the decision. He suspected a small audience was not the real reason the program was dropped.

Although the Canadian Radio Broadcasting Commission did offer some French language programming, there were complaints that private affiliates in the West often "forgot" to air these programs. In 1934, Francophones were incensed when radio in western Canada virtually ignored celebrations marking the 400th anniversary of Jacques Cartier's arrival in Canada. The Saskatchewan Branch of the Catholic Association of Canada fired off an angry letter of protest to the CRBC and the federal minister responsible for broadcasting.

There were some small victories. CKY began airing a half-hour French language show in the 1930s, and after 1936, the newly formed CBC promised more French programming in the West when it constructed a powerful new station in Watrous, Saskatchewan. The station was built, but the percentage of French on the new outlet did not come close to what Fancophone leaders had been hoping for.

Members of the newly formed Radio Ouest Française came out of the Prud'homme meeting determined to have their own stations operated by Francophones. The passion behind the movement was intense, as illustrated in a "catechism" developed by church leaders. "English radio is rapidly tending to Anglicize us," stated the document. "It is an enemy which we must fight with the same weapons. Most of the English programmes lead us to believe that life is a game of pleasure where anything is permitted. On the contrary, the few French programs we have on CBC, without actually preaching, open up a Christian atmosphere...English programs are for the most part pagan and dangerous."

The goal of Radio Ouest Française was to open four radio stations, with one in Manitoba, two in Saskatchewan and one in Alberta. Spearheading the Manitoba campaign was Father Antoine d'Eschambault of St. Boniface.

The CBC Board of Governors, the agency responsible for licensing new radio stations, reacted cautiously to the idea of a Prairie Francophone network. No, they would not issue four licences. Instead, they proposed the establishment of one French language station in St. Boniface. It would be located at 1250 on the dial with one-thousand watts of power. If that station did well, others would be considered.

Radio St. Boniface was on its way, but there were still large hurdles to overcome. Although the licence was approved in 1944, construction could not begin immediately because of a shortage of building materials caused by the war. There was also the question of money. The government had made it clear in granting the licence there would

Father Antoine d'Eschambault was instrumental in formation of CKSB.
CKSB COLLECTION: LA SOCIETE HISTORIQUE DE ST. BONIFACE.

be no financial support for the undertaking. The new station would be the property of French-speaking Catholic parishes across the province. Father d'Eschambault and colleagues like Roland Couture worked tirelessly to raise funds through "subscriptions" for the new operation. Over a two year span, $130,000 was raised. Eighty-five thousand dollars came from parishioners in Manitoba and $45,000 flowed from a fundraising campaign in Quebec.

At 6 pm, May 27, 1946, all was in readiness. From its studios at 607 Langevin Avenue, CKSB radio went on the air with the singing of O Canada. That was followed by an opening program which featured local dignitaries and a variety of Fancophone talent. The *Free Press* reported Premier Stuart Garson and St. Boniface Mayor George Maclean "reached back to the French lessons of their school days to address their listeners in that tongue." Lieutenant governor R.R. McWilliams didn't bother trying. He spoke in English. Dr. Henri Guyot, president of the new radio station, said CKSB would "try to serve

as a means of furthering understanding and tolerance between racial groups".

Among the many entertainers that evening was a 21-year-old violinist and soloist named Marie Marguerite Louisa Gisele La Fleche. Listeners could not have known that the young woman, who had been performing since she was a child, was on the cusp of stardom. From 1946 to 1950, La Fleche had her own CBC radio program called "Meet Gisele" and would have a highly successful career in Hollywood using the name Gisele Mackenzie. Her career included a long association with comedian Jack Benny. Her skill as a violinist was in sharp contrast to Benny's own musical ability and served as the perfect set-up for comedy routines. She had several hit records, appeared on the Ed Sullivan show and was a regular on a popular NBC television program known as "Your Hit Parade." For a brief period she had her own television program.

With the excitement of opening night behind them, the management and staff of CKSB were now faced with the reality of operating a radio station on a daily basis. The

French-speaking radio market was small. The Francophone population in Manitoba was only 53,000, scattered across the province. Finances were always a problem. The station lost money in its first five years of operation.

A new subscription fundraising drive was launched to raise more cash. Renting time to the CBC in the early '60s did little to improve the station's financial position, and in 1963, a third fundraising drive was launched. Faced with rising costs and a limited advertising base, the operation was sold to the Canadian Broadcasting Corporation in 1973.

While CKSB was no financial success, the station did succeed in what its founders hoped for. It was a French voice for Franco-Manitobans. Many artists, announcers and journalists heard on CKSB became known well beyond the French community...among them, fiddler Andy De Jarlis, singer and songwriter George La Fleche (brother of Giselle Mackenzie), singer Ray St. Germain, announcer Leo Remillard, journalist Renie Chartier who in the 1970s served as a senior advisor to Manitoba Premier Ed Schreyer, and writer Ron Lavallee.

Giselle La Fleche (Mackenzie) launched career at CKSB and became an internationally known recording and television star. CKSB COLLECTION: LA SOCIETE HISTORIQUE DE SAINT BONIFACE.

John Craig participating in CKX hockey broadcast. CRAIG FAMILY

End of an era

While upstart private broadcasters staked their claims in the Manitoba marketplace, political developments in other parts of the nation were about to result in a dramatic shakeup at the two radio stations owned by the Manitoba Telephone System.

CKY and CKX had operated as affiliates of the CBC network since the formation of the crown corporation in 1936. In practical terms, this meant the CBC rented time on the provincially-owned stations for network and some local programming. While the setup worked relatively well for both parties, it was hardly in line with Ottawa's radio policy flowing from the recommendations of the Aird Commission. Almost fifteen years had passed since the British Privy Council ruled that broadcasting fell exclusively under federal jurisdiction. Canada was committed to a national public broadcasting system, to be delivered through the Canadian Broadcasting Corporation. By 1946, the CBC was well on its way to establishing a network of high-powered radio stations in major centres across the country. Given the circumstances, the question was obvious. Why was one province still in the broadcasting business? CKY and CKX had become, as Premier Garson put it, "a constitutional embarrassment for national radio policy."

The nascent stirring of Quebec nationalism brought the issue to a head. In the final year of the war, the government of Maurice Duplessis passed broadcasting legislation giving the Quebec government the power to set up its own radio stations. While Quebec took no immediate steps to get into the business, it was a troubling development for advocates of a national public broadcasting system and a clear challenge to federal authority. Saskatchewan and Alberta were also considering their own radio stations.

The federal response was definitive. C.D. Howe, the Minister Responsible for Broadcasting, informed the House of Commons "the government has decided that, since broadcasting is the sole responsibility of the dominion government, broadcast licences shall not be issued to other governments, or corporations owned by other governments."

The policy sealed the fate of both CKY and CKX. The Manitoba government was stuck. Talks with Ottawa and the CBC dragged on for months, but in the end the province was left with no choice but to divest itself of a money-making enterprise.

In a radio address in December of 1947, Premier Garson informed listeners that CKY and CKX were on the auction block. The CBC had already made an undisclosed offer for CKY that would act as a reserve bid. CKX would be sold to the highest bidder.

The CBC had also been assigned the AM 990 frequency being used by CKY. If the CBC bid was unsuccessful, it would use that spot on the dial and build its own high-powered station.

Should CKY be sold to a private company, it would be assigned a frequency of 1080.

The Premier concluded that "the province was stepping out of the broadcasting field which hadn't cost taxpayers a dollar... whatever purchase money the province would get would be additional profit for the taxpayers over and above that already received."

While CKY had an obvious buyer in the CBC, the sale of CKX radio in Brandon was more problematic. Brandon, with a population of 20,000, was a small radio market heavily dependent on the state of the agricultural community surrounding it. The peaks and valleys of farm commodity prices would always be felt at the radio station. While usually able to turn a profit, CKX was by no means a cash cow like CKY.

The one man who wanted to purchase the station didn't have the money, but that was not going to stop Johnny Craig, who, in one way or the other, had been associated with CKX since 1938.

At age seven, young Johnny had come to Canada from Scotland. His father was an undertaker who thought he could make a better life running a dairy farm at Virden. Johnny grew up milking cows and doing farm chores. Like most prairie boys, he learned to skate at an early age, and at 17 was tending goal for the Virden senior hockey team. His rapier reflexes soon caught the attention of hockey men in Brandon, and in 1925, Johnny joined the Brandon senior hockey team...at the time one of the more competitive clubs in the country. Little did he realize hockey would be his passport to a future broadcasting career.

An injury and a bout of scarlet fever effectively ended his hockey days, but Craig was already looking to the world of business. He took a job at a fledgling automobile dealership in Brandon. His quick smile and gregarious personality made him a natural for selling. By 1928, he had his own garage and automobile business called Craig Motors. The business, located on 10th Street in Brandon, got off to a good start but the Depression put tremendous financial pressure on the Craig family. Demand for cars and gasoline plummeted. A baby had also arrived in 1933, named Andrew Stuart. To help boost his income, Craig took a part-time job as commercial manager at CKX. As part of his efforts, he convinced a client to sponsor a hockey broadcast featuring a game between Brandon and St. Boniface. The idea created an immediate problem in

that CKX had no one to do play-by-play. John would have to do the job himself.

As it turned out, John Craig was a very good hockey broadcaster. "Although he had never broadcast before," reported *Manitoba Calling*, "his effort was voted among the best hockey stories ever heard."

World War II brought more complications for Craig Motors. With fuel and rubber rationed, and automobile manufacturing curtailed, Craig was left with no choice but to close his operation. He went to work for the Victory Loans program and again witnessed the power of radio to raise cash. At one point he even had loud speakers attached to the bottom of a fighter plane, which then flew at very low altitude over western Manitoba with CKX blaring the virtues of Victory Bonds and latest totals of money raised to help fight the war.

With the end of the conflict, Craig's fortunes suddenly changed. He re-opened his service station and was able to obtain the rights to sell Nash cars in western Manitoba. For a time, a "Nash" was the only new vehicle available in the area. Because

auto manufacturers had been required to turn their assembly lines to military use, Canadians had not had access to new cars in almost six years. Craig's business took off. He had a waiting list for new vehicles and was able to command top dollar. The Craig family had never been so financially secure. It did not mean, however, that John Craig had the money to buy a radio station.

When word came that CKX was for sale, Craig's entrepreneurial instincts kicked in. He recognized the potential in such an investment. In its entire history, CKX had lost money only once and that was in the heart of the Depression. In the previous business year, it had recorded a profit. Utilizing contacts built up over the years, Craig began putting together a community group that would offer to purchase the government-owned station. He travelled to towns and municipalities around Brandon, drumming up support. In the end, there were a number of small investors and a syndicate of seven that made the offer to purchase. In addition to Craig, the group included Dr. H.O. McDiarmid, Alexander

Start here ↓

Boyd, Edmund Fotheringham, Harold Smith, James Rust and N.W. Kerr.

It turned out to be the only serious bid, and early in January of 1948, it was officially announced that Craig and his group were successful. CKX had been purchased for $65,000.

When it came to business, John Craig ran a tight ship. One of his first acts as the new owner was to get rid of six of the station's 23 employees and then boost the sales staff. In its first year as a private radio station, profits jumped by 20 percent.

One of John Craig's early hires was a reporter from the *Winnipeg Tribune* named Jim Keilback. His job was to cover sports in the region. Keilback had barely taken up his post in Brandon when son Curt was born. The name Keilback would become well-known among sports fans across the province. Jim took his broadcasting talents to CJOB, CKY, and eventually Yorkton, Saskatchewan. When Curt was 11 years old, his father let him take the mic and handle play-by-play of a senior hockey game in Saskatchewan. "You could see the signs that

he knew what he was doing," says Jim. From 1979 to 2007, Curt was the play-by-play voice of the Winnipeg Jets and Phoenix Coyotes of the National Hockey League.

Over time, John Craig, along with son Stuart, would add FM radio and bring television to Brandon, ultimately building a regional communications network serving much of rural Manitoba.

Back in Winnipeg, no one was surprised when, in January of 1948, Premier Garson announced CKY had been bought by the Canadian Broadcasting Corporation. The purchase price was $200,000, an amount no private broadcaster could compete with.

Over the next few months, CBC revved up while CKY wound down. Work on a new 570 foot tower and transmitter building moved full speed ahead on land the CBC had purchased just east of Carman. The crown corporation had committed to incorporate as many CKY staff as possible into its new operation. Regardless, there was uncertainty among CKY employees as to where they would end up and what they might be doing. Musicians and actors who

had been part of CKY programming would also have to wait and see how they might fit into CBC plans. One casualty was the MTS radio publication *Manitoba Calling*. It would cease operation.

At CKY, there were parties with numerous individual achievements to be recognized...among them, University of Manitoba professor A. Jackson who had delivered 813 fifteen-minute nature talks on CKY; Lillian Shaw, undisputedly the first female announcer in Manitoba, and perhaps in Canada; and actor George Waight, who at the end of his career estimated he had appeared in over 2,000 radio plays, a significant percentage of them on CKY.

On July 1, 1948, dignitaries arrived for a ceremony that would see CKY radio officially transferred to the CBC. The final words on the Manitoba government radio station were hardly eloquent. Premier Garson, who was to pass the torch to the CBC, botched his few lines badly. He transposed the call letters and misread his script. After some nervous laughter, the invited dignitaries were relieved when the crisp

elocution of Maurice Burchell flowed over the airwaves. "This is CBW Winnipeg." CKY was no more. The CBC had fully arrived in Manitoba.

The New CKY

As it turned out, the call letters CKY did not disappear for long. In less than a year, plans for a new privately-owned CKY were in the works. Saskatchewan native Lloyd Moffat was looking to Winnipeg to expand his radio holdings. At age 40, Moffat was a veteran of the radio business, having established and operated radio station CKBI in Prince Albert since 1933. Radio was in its formative stages when Moffat was growing up in Regina. As a youngster he would build radio sets. After moving to Prince Albert, he became leader of a local radio club which, for several years, operated as a non-commercial radio station. He later turned it into a commercial operation.

The new CKY billed itself as a powerful new voice in Winnipeg and Manitoba.

Indeed, the 5,000-watt radio station was built to reach as wide an audience as possible. The most visible features of the new station were the three 230-foot towers located at the transmitter site just northwest of St. Agathe. The tri-tower setup was the only one of its kind in Manitoba and one of very few in Canada. According to the station's advertising, CKY could reach some 300,000 homes within its coverage area.

The resurrection of the historic call letters CKY was the direct result of the new station's spot on the radio dial. With the CBC now in command of the 990 frequency, the 1080 spot on the AM dial was left open, as no private company had won the tender to buy the Manitoba government station. A year and a half later, Moffat requested and received a license for the 1080 frequency, so it seemed only fitting the new private station be called CKY.

The CKY offices, studios and control room occupied 6,000 square feet on the second floor of the London building at 432 Main Street. Moffat had purchased two grand pianos, and the station's main studio was large enough to "accommodate a full orchestra or a large cast for dramatic performances." CKY also claimed "a musical transcription library larger than any of its kind in Manitoba."

Marquee voices on the original staff included Ed McCrea, who had previously worked at CKRC; Doug Whelan, a veteran broadcaster from Saskatchewan, who was the morning man; and John O'Leary, a specialist in dramatic narration. O'Leary would go on to a high profile career as an announcer on the CBC network. The first news director was an Irishman named Jack Sweeny who had begun his media career delivering newspapers in Dublin. After emigrating to Winnipeg, he went to work at the *Free Press*. Among his staff was a young newscaster named Ed Derback, who would become one of the premiere news readers on CBW Winnipeg throughout the 1970s and '80s.

Having famous call letters was no guarantee of success. The station "had to struggle desperately to gain an audience," recalled Pat McDougal, who was part of the station's original staff. CKY developed local programs such as a regular feature on Manitoba communities. Programs like Hopalong Cassidy and Guy Lombardo were also popular. By now, however, local radio was more fragmented than ever before. It was not until CKY boosted its power and changed its frequency to 580 that the station began to take off.

As the clock ticked down to 1950, the Manitoba radio landscape had been altered significantly. In only four years, the number of stations in Winnipeg had jumped from two to five, provincial ownership of radio was no more, the CBC had fully arrived and CKX in Brandon was now in the hands of private operators. The stations of the 1940s would become Manitoba's heritage radio stations. Over time, they would re-invent themselves and spawn new broadcasting enterprises. Decades later, very different stations with corporate owners and fancy brands would trace their roots to these original six.

CHAPTER SIX

Torrents and Tragedy

From a community service perspective, the great flood of 1950 was local radio's finest hour. Although radio stations were no more prepared for the magnitude of the flood than anyone else, they adapted quickly and became the vital communications link in the battle against the rising Red River. Never had listening to the radio been so important.

May 3, 1950 was a dreary Wednesday. Winnipeggers hearing the forecast could only shake their heads and wonder what was to come. The Dominion Weather Bureau was calling for heavy rain and strong winds over the next twenty-four hours. To the south, the Red River Valley was already a massive lake with most farms and communities evacuated. The dikes protecting Winnipeg were holding, but just barely.

The rain and the winds did come. By Friday, eight dikes had given way to the pressure of the waves. Winnipeg was headed for a full-scale disaster. At a midnight meeting at the Legislature, Premier Douglas Campbell huddled with his senior flood advisers. It was agreed the military, under the leadership of Brigadier R.E.A. Morton, would take command of the flood fight. Evacuation plans were put in place.

Radio stations would be called upon to provide up-to-the-minute information. Brigadier Morton urged Manitobans to keep their radios on "constantly," to keep abreast of emergency measures.

Never had Winnipeg broadcasters faced such responsibility. Radio stations went on the air 24 hours a day. Three blasts from an old siren at the *Free Press* building would signal a dike had been breached. Radio was expected to provide the details. The propinquity of the radio stations to the *Free Press* was of considerable value. Winnipeg's five English language stations were within a few blocks of each other in the downtown. Regular programming was tossed out the window. In some instances, advertising time was surrendered to make

Opposite: CBC's Maurice Burchell reporting live from rowboat during 1950 flood.
MANITOBA ARCHIVES

way for flood information. On May 6, the *Free Press* reported that radio stations "were interrupting programs with flood bulletins, information on dike conditions, appeals for equipment and volunteers and messages from authorities. They are acting as clearing houses for volunteer workers and organizations which offer assistance and at all times are in close touch with army, Red Cross and civic officials."

Winnipeg broadcasters were hardly immune from the rising flood waters. At 9 pm on May 5, CKRC listeners heard the station go silent. Water had burst through a dike in south Winnipeg, shorting out the station's transmitter. Chief engineer Bert Hooper and his staff worked valiantly into the night, coming up with a makeshift fix that had the station back on the air by 2:30 am.

The CKRC transmitter site, located on an elevated piece of land near St. Norbert, was surrounded by a sea of floodwater. For the next nine days, Hooper and two other technicians lived on the small island, fighting to keep the equipment dry and the station on the air. During that time the sliver

of land became a clearing point for evacuees, a supply depot and dock for military boats. "The whole area is desolated," wrote Hooper in a dispatch to Canadian Press. "We saw cows and horses in barns with just their heads above water. Dogs on dry places were howling their heads off. That's an awful noise to listen to for eight days...I think the worst thing though was an old man near the station. He was living in his loft...no stock, no nothing. But he wasn't leaving. He said 'this is all I've got'."

In the end, Hooper and his crew were forced to give up as the dikes could not hold back the water. To stay on the air, CKRC activated emergency equipment on top of the *Free Press* building which had been rushed in from Regina. "I'm so tired I can hardly talk," wrote Hopper.

CJOB was facing a similar challenge. Its transmitter near Whittier Park in St. Boniface was quickly engulfed by the flood. Again, it was the work of a tireless engineering staff headed by Reg Drurie that kept the radio station going. A hole was cut in the roof of the building so that

equipment could be raised and kept dry. With water three-quarters of the way up the side of the facility, CJOB staffers pitched a tent on the roof and stayed at the site. Even Jack Blick took his turn on top of the transmitter building.

On Portage Avenue East, flood waters crept to within 150 yards of the heavily sandbagged MTS building which housed CBC studios. Pumps ran 24 hours a day, shooting out water that seeped into the basement of the building. The main worry was a loss of power, and CBC engineers set up an emergency power supply ready for immediate activation if required.

Virtually every employee at every radio station was called in to help the cause. Sleep was at a premium, with staffers often bunking at the radio stations during the peak of the flood. More than a few broadcasters were facing threats to their own property. The *Free Press* reported that "most (radio staffs) put in long hours on dikes after their regular work."

On May 10, CBW reported "the greatest mass evacuation in Canadian history is underway." Before it was over, 100,000 people would be moved, with property damage running into the hundreds of millions of dollars. The Red River flood had become news around the world.

Of the many services radio provided, it was the personal connections which proved the medium's greatest strength. In the sometimes chaotic conditions, people would disappear or lose contact with family or loved ones. Newspapers reported radio stations were receiving "thousands of personal calls. These messages have included offers for accommodations from relatives all across Canada, long lists of telegrams piling up for untraceable Manitobans, pleas for dike workers to return home to evacuate their own families and for teenagers whose parents have not seen them in days." Women would prepare food for those working on the dikes. When it was ready, they would call a radio station. Soon a car would come by to pick up and deliver. CJOB ran newspaper ads simply stating "Call Us—Anytime for Anything. If We Can We Will Help."

It could have been the motto for any Winnipeg radio station.

Seldom mentioned, but not without significance, is the role radio played in stress relief. In those horrible days as residents sought to save their city, there was little time for relaxation. Movie theatres closed, concerts were cancelled and even a number of beer parlours and clubs temporarily shut down.

Radio was the only entertainment available. While stations provided emergency coverage they also attempted to maintain regular programming as best they could, with music, dramas and sitcoms. Comedian Bob Hope mentioned the Manitoba flood on his popular network program, urging listeners to do whatever they could to help. CJOB morning man Cliff Gardner tried to bring some levity to the whole mess by adapting popular songs of the day with flood lyrics . The hit song "If I Knew You Were Coming I'd Have Baked a Cake" became "If I knew you were coming I'd have built a dike." Or "chuck another sandbag, sandbag, sandbag," to the tune of "Music, Music, Music."

Flood Relief

When the waters finally began to recede in mid-May, radio shifted into the mode of fundraiser for flood relief. Given the magnitude of the crisis, the requirements were immense. A hundred thousand people had been evacuated, acres of the city were underwater, 10,000 homes were destroyed and 5,000 other buildings damaged. According to Manitoba government estimates, flood damage totalled over $125 million (or over one billion dollars in 2012 funds).

The Manitoba Flood Relief Fund was set up in response to the many individuals and organizations offering help. Radio was the medium to publicize the cause. On May 14, virtually every radio station in the country broadcast a 20-minute segment describing the flood, its impact and the need for financial support. Local stations worked together, although in the midst of it all CJOB was able to pull off a small coup, much to the chagrin of its competitors. One of the world's best-known entertainers.

Gracie Fields, had been scheduled for a Winnipeg concert in May. Because of the flood it had to be postponed. On Tuesday evening, May 17, Fields made a quick visit to the city anyway, to hand over a personal donation of $1,000 for flood relief. "Get the muck cleared away," Gracie urged, "before I come back next month." The only station to broadcast the event live was CJOB.

In Toronto, two former Winnipeg radio employees were organizing a broadcasting extravaganza aimed at raising big money for flood relief. Waldo Holden, who had worked at CKRC, was now sales manager at CFRB. Hugh Newton, a public relations man, had been at CKRC and CKY when it was owned by the Manitoba Telephone System. Under their leadership, the "Flood the Fund" radio show became a reality. Other Winnipeg broadcasting expatriates jumped in to help out. The list included Jack Dennett, Jack Scott, Beth Lockerbie and George Murray. The live event was held at Maple Leaf Gardens. Owner Conn Smythe provided the facility for the broadcast. Nearly 15,000 people jammed into the

hockey shrine to hear a veritable who's who of the entertainment industry. Among those volunteering their time were British comedian George Formby, Sir Ernest MacMillan and the 100-member Toronto Symphony Orchestra, singer Giselle Mackenzie, Fred Waring and his Pennsylvanians orchestra, The Leslie Bell Singers and tenor George Murray. Hosting the event was star of stage and screen, Jack Carson, who had been born in Carman, Manitoba. Between 7:30 and 9 pm on May 26, local listeners had no choice in what they heard. Every station in the province carried the "Flood the Fund" broadcast from Maple Leaf Gardens. So too did every station in Canada, public and private. The program was carried live by the Mutual Broadcasting network in the United States and recorded and made available to ABC affiliate stations. In all, the broadcast aired on 729 radio stations in North America with portions also heard on the BBC.

Listeners were urged to donate to the Manitoba Flood Relief Fund. Those attending the Toronto event contributed $25,000

to the cause. On May 26, the day of the broadcast, contributions to the Fund stood at $1.8 million. A week later, it had grown by nearly a million dollars. All totalled, the Manitoba Flood Relief Fund raised nearly 10 million dollars.

Radio's work during the flood became a model for future emergencies, such as the blizzards of 1966 and 1986, and "The Flood of the Century" in 1997. Despite the emergence of new mediums, radio remained the most immediate mechanism for dispensing information in a crisis. Whether guiding a snowmobile to deliver medical supplies or directing sandbaggers to a threatened property, radio served as a central agency connecting people. In an emergency, that has always been its strength.

Disaster

Less than two years after the flood, the nation's attention was again focused on Manitoba, this time because of the worst tragedy in radio broadcasting history.

Downed CBC tower at Carman. CBC

Near noon on February 4, 1952, an RCAF C-45 Beechcraft aircraft swept low near Carman. It was one of 11 planes heading for Winnipeg from an RCAF flight training school at Stevenson's airbase. Conditions for flying were terrible as a thick fog had enveloped the area. As the craft swung northward, its altitude was less than 500 feet. Only a mile and a half east of town, just north of Highway #3, the aircraft twisted wildly as the pilot lost control. The plane plowed into a farmer's field, bursting into flames. All three men on board the training flight were killed.

The aircraft had clipped a guy wire of the CBC transmitter tower. The 570-foot structure was now tilting precariously. Remarkably, CBW radio stayed on the air. Inside the main transmitter building, two CBC employees did not even realize the transmitter had been hit. Only when a farmer passing by pounded on the door did they rush out to witness the carnage. As RCMP, fire crews and emergency vehicles rushed to the site, CBC engineers and technicians headed to the scene. Workers

THE VICTIMS IN CANADA'S WORST BROADCASTING TRAGEDY

Carman, Manitoba. February 4 and 5, 1952.

Air-crash:

RCAF-Flight officer **Charles Chow-Leong ,** age 29, Lethbridge, Alberta

RCAF-Student airman **Peter Frederick Harvey,** age 20, Cambridgeshire, England

RCAF-Student airman **Edward Scanlan,** age 18, Chiswick, London, England

Tower collapse:

Walter Burtnyk, age 28, Alfred Avenue, Winnipeg. Walter was married with a six-and-a-half-month old child.

Jake A. Dyck, age 23, Spence Street, Winnipeg

Ronald Erickson, age 19, Tyndall, Manitoba. "Ronnie" was known as an excellent hockey player.

All three victims in the tower collapse were employed by the Dominion Bridge Company in Winnipeg.

from Dominion Bridge were also notified; their job would be to shore up the transmitter tower.

"It was so foggy you couldn't see the first guy lights," recalled Joe Knowles, who worked at the transmitter. In the midst of the turmoil, a second aircraft came within a whisker of hitting the tower. Again, this aircraft was flying exceptionally low. According to newspaper accounts from eye-witnesses, the pilot, noticing the structure looming in front of him, banked the craft sideways at the last second and manoeuvred between the guy wires and the tower.

By mid-afternoon, Dominion Bridge workers were on the scene. Before anything could be done to straighten the tower, a new guy wire would have to be attached to rein-force the structure. Night was falling and floodlights were brought in to illuminate the worksite. Even with the bright lights the disastrous events of the day weighed heavily. The Dominion Bridge employees took a break knowing the most danger-ous part of their task was still ahead. They sipped coffee and munched on donuts in the transmitter building while engaging in a bit of macabre humor. Someone suggested there was perhaps a need for life insurance.

Near midnight, all was in readiness. Three men began to make their way up the tower. There are conflicting reports about what happened next. Some people describe a calm February night, with only intermittent gusts of wind. According to a *Free Press* account, "the danger of high winds in the area which might damage the (CBC) structure was believed to be behind the urgency with which the crew swung into action after midnight." The men climbed up a ladder inside the structure. According to one eyewitness account, the first worker was nearing the top of the tower, the second was about 500 feet up, while the third was at the 250-foot mark. The wind picked up and a light at the top of the tower wavered ever so slightly. Then came a sickening grinding sound as the 85-ton tower collapsed in two directions. The dozen or so people on the ground scrambled for their lives, some running northward at top speed, while others dove under cars and trucks. The lights were out, and in the darkness men screamed and yelled trying to locate co-workers. Not all voices were heard. The three men who had been on the tower were dead.

Sirens could be heard in the dead of night as police and emergency vehicles rushed to the CBC transmitter tower for the second time in just 12 hours. As might be expected, the next few hours were chaotic. CBC technician Joe Knowles drove back to Carman and started knocking on the doors of people he knew. "I was trying to find liquor," recalled Knowles "for the remaining (Dominion Bridge) crew. We had two or three drinks and put them to bed in the transmitter building because they were just broke-up." Of the six men killed, all were under age 30. Two were teenagers.

Later, CBC employee Ross Elliot remembered the darkness. He and several colleagues arrived at the scene minutes after the tower came down. The structure with its top-to-bottom lights had been a landmark, the highest point on the Prairies. CBW was off the air and would remain silent for the next 54 hours. It meant the local station was unable to provide breaking news coverage of the death of King George VI and the ascension of his daughter Elizabeth II as Queen. Radio stations CKY and CKRC picked up national CBC programming.

Eventually, a makeshift antenna or long wire served to get the station operating again. By the end of the summer, work was well underway on a new, smaller structure. The disaster taught many lessons about flight planning, pilot training, worker safety and the vulnerability of radio broadcasting. By law, the transmitter site had to be manned 24 hours a day. During the height of the cold war, a bomb shelter was constructed at the Carman location. The facility was complete with beds, food, water supply and the technical equipment to broadcast directly from the bunker in the event of nuclear attack. In 1964, the Carman transmitter sent out its last signal as the CBC moved its facilities to a more modern structure near Starbuck.

CHAPTER SEVEN

Rural Roots

Early in 1950 came rumblings of a radio station for Dauphin. By broadcasting standards, the community was small. Dauphin's population was just over 5,000, although it served a broad hinterland of farms and agricultural communities. Spearheading the efforts to launch the station was Ken Parton, a broadcasting executive from Yorkton radio who had moved to Dauphin. With him came George Gallagher, who had served as sales manager in Yorkton.

Raising the capital to get the venture off the ground proved problematic. Parton and his colleagues beat the bushes in Dauphin and the surrounding area, drumming up investors and potential advertisers. The CBC licensing board deferred an initial application because of concern that financing was not in place. In the end, the Dauphin Broadcasting Company would claim over 100 shareholders, among them some prominent members of the local Ukrainian community. They included Dr. Michael Potoski, who had begun his medical practice in Sifton before moving to Dauphin; Thomas "Tommy" Warnock, a prominent lawyer and well-known Liberal; and businessmen S. Zaplitny and J.L. Tycholitz. The other known investors were William Cruise, Mrs. W.G. Peebles, W.J. Ward, C.A. McNiven, Joe Maillard, R.P. Scott and C.J. Steele. The application to operate CKDM was finally approved in late fall. It would be the first English language radio station in the province where many of the principal owners were not of British heritage.

As Dauphin residents finished up their final preparations for Christmas, CKDM was scrambling to get on the air. Technical problems had slowed plans for an opening launch. Station management scheduled a test broadcast for December 22 to ensure all was ready. At that time, a start date for regular programming would be announced. In describing that first broadcast, the *Dauphin Herald* couldn't resist a bit of hyperbole. "This is CKDM Dauphin,

Opposite: Live on Location: CFAM farm service. GOLDEN WEST BROADCASTING

Manitoba...these first words of the infant radio station came clear and strong...the occasion was something of a thrill for local folks, resembling the first words of their own infants." CKDM began regular programming on January 5, 1951 at 1230 on the AM dial, with 250 watts of power. Studios were located on Third Avenue. The station had a staff of six. Ken Parton was general manager, George Gallagher served as sales manager and also read the news. Jack Henderson was production manager, William Portman chief announcer, Peter Prosdoswech, a local hired as an announcer/operator, and Nettie Fersiuk, secretary.

Those early days were difficult for the fledgling station. Management and the board of directors clashed repeatedly over the direction of the operation. Manager Ken Parton was gone a month after CKDM opened. George Gallagher departed a short time later. "We certainly had growing pains," recalled Gallagher in an interview years later.

With the station on the air, there was no turning back. Although resources may have been scarce, CKDM covered local events, agricultural news, sports, and offered an outlet for local entertainers in the predominately Ukrainian community. Over time, CKDM would play an important role in the understanding and promotion of Ukrainian culture in the province. Company president Tommy Warnock had been born in Ukraine. Both Warnock and his wife were active in the local cultural community and saw to it that Ukrainian events were well promoted.

Another of CKDM's early investors was local businessman Basil Lazeruk. But it was Lazeruk's daughter, not his business dealing, that most interested young announcer Jack Henderson. The attraction turned out to be mutual. In 1951, Helen Lazeruk, a school teacher, married Henderson. Before long, Helen would be an "on-air" personality in her own right, doing a homemaking show and offering advice to others thinking of marriage. However, it was a 1960s program called "Songs and Music of the Ukraine" that carved a special place in broadcasting history for Helen Henderson. She was the only female broadcaster at that time to produce and announce her own program in the Ukrainian language, outside Ukraine. The station would have been hard pressed to find anyone better qualified to produce the show as Helen was a longtime director of the Greek Orthodox Church Choir and the National Ukrainian Festival Choir. "We always had Ukrainian," recalls Rene Maillard, President of Dauphin Broadcasting Limited, whose father was a founding member of CKDM. "When it came to funeral announcements or a Christmas time, Ukrainian mass, we always had announcers that could speak in Ukrainian."

It took a Maritimer from Windsor, Nova Scotia to finally get CKDM established as a profitable enterprise. Hugh Dunlop arrived in Dauphin in 1961 to take up the position of General Manager. He would hold the job for the next 26 years. A trained lawyer, Dunlop had the communication skills and community-mindedness to sell the radio station. "Hugh was a real gentleman," says Rene Maillard. "He had to take the station and completely revamp it to get it going. I don't think the station had been doing that well financially up until Hugh came in and then it started to get out of the red." During his time in Dauphin, Dunlop not only ran the station but also served two terms as mayor. Covering city hall was a must, and no doubt more than a little intimidating for the CKDM news staff.

Dauphin and CKDM became known across North America in early 1970 because of an article in *Sports Illustrated* magazine. The story chronicled one of the ugliest hockey playoff series in local history as the Dauphin Kings took on the Kenora Muskies in Kenora. The battle took place not only on the ice but in the stands. Irate Kenora fans hurled eggs, dead fish and even a chicken at Dauphin players. Future NHL goaltender Ron Lowe estimated he was hit by debris at least eight times. CKDM was caught in the middle. According to the article, a group of Kenora fans taunted a contingent from Dauphin that had travelled to the Ontario town. The abuse and threats grew increasingly violent as Kenora fans turned their anger on CKDM and play-by-play announcer Bernie Basaraba. With no

protection and some of the foulest language ever to hit the airwaves, Basaraba shut down the broadcast temporarily until some semblance of order was restored.

The conclusion of the match did not end the trouble. With fears mounting that Dauphin fans would retaliate when the series moved back to their hometown, Mayor Dunlop took to the CKDM airwaves appealing for calm. As a further precaution, he called in the RCMP to provide additional police protection. In the end, the game was played with no further complications. Yet that one short hockey series gave CKDM radio more exposure than it could ever have imagined.

Veteran Yorkton television broadcaster Linus Westberg took over the general manager's post in 1987 when Hugh Dunlop stepped down because of illness. He passed away a short time later. The foundation he had laid paved the way for Westberg to significantly expand CKDM's operation in the Parklands region.

Like most smaller radio stations, CKDM was a starting point for many young

broadcasters who went on to successful careers. Not many stations, however, can claim an employee who spawned an entirely new radio station.

CFRY

One of the first engineers at CKDM was a young Dauphin resident named Richard Digby Hughes. As a youngster, Hughes was an inquisitive lad. By Grade 8 he had built his first single tube radio receiver. At age 15, he had an amateur radio licence. He set up a shop fixing electrical appliances, including radios, and with the outbreak of war, served as a wireless radio mechanic for the RCAF. At CKDM he was described in one newspaper article as "the man who kept the radio station on the air."

Looking south, Hughes' entrepreneurial spirit kicked in. The city of Portage la Prairie was bigger than Dauphin, surrounded by rich agricultural land and only 50 miles from Winnipeg. And it had no radio station. Hughes sensed an opportunity.

In applying for a licence, he noted that "Portage is one of the rare cities in Canada without the services of local radio. The fact it supports two weekly and one daily newspaper is a definite indication of the size and support of a local audience." To further bolster his case, Hughes argued that "because of competition, stations in Winnipeg cannot program for rural areas."

On May 2, 1956, 2,100 kilometres from Portage, a federally-appointed Commission was holding hearings on the future of Canadian broadcasting. Among those participating at the Ottawa summit was Winnipegger Roy J. Fry. A former advertising executive of the T. Eaton Company, Fry had been appointed several years earlier as western representative of the CBC Board of Governors. He would never return to Manitoba. Fry suffered a heart attack that Wednesday and died in an Ottawa hospital. Digby Hughes was shocked. In the process of preparing his licensing application, Hughes had received considerable help from Fry and the two had developed a close working relationship. Hughes felt the loss

deeply and telephoned Fry's widow, promising to name his new radio station after her husband. Whatever call letters Hughes originally had in mind were dropped. The Portage la Prairie radio station would be known as CFRY.

CFRY went on the air October 18 at 1570 on the dial, with 250 watts of power. As the single owner, Hughes was in full control, although he was far from the stereotypical broadcast executive. He was hardly rich and was ready to use his own hands to build the station. Along with son Richard (better known as "Red"), he did much of the physical work to get the station operational, including assembling the transmitter tower. Studios were located in a few rooms of the Portage Hotel on Saskatchewan Avenue. Before moving his family from Dauphin, Hughes lived in a room upstairs. Daughter Sandy remembers stories about her father having to borrow money from friends to meet payroll.

If Digby Hughes had any concerns about the size of his listening audience, those worries were dispelled on the station's first

Digby Hughes wrapping cake mix for CFRY's first birthday promotion. SANDRA BAZIN

anniversary. Gauging listener response turned out to be a piece of cake. To mark its first year on the air, CFRY promised that anyone who sent a card would receive a birthday cake in the form of a Five Roses cake mix package. Each package weighed one pound, and the station had received half a ton or a thousand boxes to give away. Response was overwhelming.

CFRY received 1,459 birthday wishes. It took three people two full days to package each cake mix, along with a birthday candle. The total mailing cost was nearly $150, not an insignificant sum for a fledgling business in 1957. The cake caper, however, garnered the radio station immeasurable good will, and presumably some long-term advertising revenue from the Five Roses Flour Company.

A year later, CFRY moved from its cramped quarters in the Portage Hotel to new facilities at 1500 Saskatchewan Avenue, which would serve as the station's home for the next 46 years. Like every other rural radio station in western Canada, good times and bad times were tied directly to the cyclical nature of the agricultural economy. By 1961, the station had switched to 920 on the dial and boosted its power to 1,000 watts. Richard "Red" Hughes obtained a degree in engineering and business administration from the University of North Dakota, and would eventually take over responsibility for managing the company.

Agriculture, sports and country music became the mainstay of the Portage station. Agriculture director Howard Barker served local farmers for nearly 40 years. Another veteran staffer was John Aune, who started in 1960, and with the exception of a stint as a disc jockey in Regina, could still be heard on the station 50 years later. While there was no shortage of rough on-air moments, CFRY served as a training ground for numerous young broadcasters who would go on to very successful careers elsewhere. Newscaster Vic Edwards worked in several major markets across the country, Brian Barkley became Winnipeg's best known traffic reporter, Alex Docking emerged as network television reporter with CTV, Darryl Provost rocked the airwaves as a disc jockey in Winnipeg and Montreal, DJ John Murphy would become a member of the Canadian Country Music Hall of Fame and announcer John Harvard would end up as Lieutenant Governor of Manitoba.

CFRY would become the first radio station in Canada to simulcast programming on AM and FM; it also broke new ground in hiring the province's first female sports director and play-by-play hockey broadcaster. Winnipegger Bev Lockhart made hockey history in 1977 at CKSW in Swift Current when she became the first woman to call a hockey game. It garnered her national recognition including an appearance on the CBC's iconic television program "Front Page Challenge." Shortly afterward, Red Hughes hired Lockhart to broadcast Portage Terrier hockey games for a number of seasons. "I think people raised an eyebrow (as to) why he would bring in a girl to do sports," recalls Lockhart (married name Edmondson). "I did eight years of Portage Terrier hockey." She later became CFRY's program director.

While some stations flipped formats with regularity, CFRY remained true to country music from day one. "There's lots of country between rock and talk" was a one-time CFRY slogan. The Hughes men had definite opinions about the genre. Vic Edwards recalls "Red" yanking a Gordon Lightfoot record off a turntable. "I think it was not that he didn't have any use for Gordon Lightfoot," says Bev Edmondson. "He didn't feel it was country, he thought it was too folksy for us to play." CFRY was indeed country. Smack in the middle between Manitoba's two largest urban centres, the station never lost its unique rural qualities, and as a result, gave voice to a region often neglected by big city broadcasters.

CFAM

By 1957, 150 kilometres southeast of Portage, a very different type of radio station was taking shape. A group of Mennonites had been granted a licence to start a radio station in Altona. While pledging to serve all in the region, the shareholders were equally determined the station would reflect the values and faith of the predominately Mennonite community that stretched from Morden to Steinbach. Provisional guidelines set down by the original owners made it evident CFAM would be a unique radio station. The goals were lofty. The new station would:

"Provide radio listening to our constituency that is not only in accordance but magnifies and is a witness of our Christian faith as we understand it in the framework of our Mennonite principles and doctrines.

It shall also reach out to all people in clear and uncompromising testimony the good news of the gospel of Jesus Christ, preaching salvation through repentance, belief in Jesus as Lord and Saviour, in the necessity of being born again, of justification through faith, sanctification, the discipleship of the believer and in a believer's church.

It shall present the best in all that it offers, such as music, drama, speeches, current events, worship services etc. Jazz, swing, crime stories, anything that is demoralizing or degrading is absolutely forbidden; cheap comedy & music such as westerns etc. should be discouraged as much as possible.

Advertising should be controlled by the board. It shall be clean and honest, and only of such things we can subscribe to in good conscience. We cannot connive with or be a party to dishonest or misleading advertising claims."

Abram J. Thiessen was the driving force behind efforts to get the station off the ground. He had grown up on a farm in Rosenfeld, near Altona. As a young man, he had hoped to become a missionary but couldn't afford the cost of the required education. In the early 1930s, he began hauling eggs and chickens to Winnipeg in his grandfather's car. He would also take passengers for 75 cents one way. From those modest beginnings would emerge a business empire that included both Thiessen and Grey Goose bus lines. A.J. Thiessen was the principal investor in CFAM. Other key investors included David K. Friesen, who ran a printing and publishing company, and Walter Kroeker, who owned a

Opening night at CFAM. Left to right
Les Garside, Dennis Barkman, and Reuben
Hamm. GOLDEN WEST BROADCASTING

seed company. Other than perhaps being involved in some church programs, none of the investors had any background in radio. For expertise they turned to veteran broadcaster Les Garside, who ran Inland Broadcasting in Winnipeg. Garside's career dated back to the 1920s when he worked for the Richardsons at CJRW. He would serve as consultant at the new station for a year.

With much fanfare, CFAM went on the air March 13, 1957. Premier D.L. Campbell was among the dignitaries welcoming the new radio station. No fewer than six different languages were spoken during the inaugural broadcast: English, German, French, Icelandic, Ukrainian and Hebrew. Among the eleven new hires on hand that night was a bespectacled 19-year-old who had been taken on to write commercial copy. Not long out of high school, Elmer Hildebrand was best known in the community as a hockey goaltender. "I was still living on the farm but I knew I wasn't going to be a farmer," he recalls. "I had no idea what I would do after high school and then the radio station started to develop and I applied...My experience in listening to radio was Saturday night hockey with Foster Hewitt." No one could have predicted that this rather shy and soft-spoken young man would go on to shape the company into a multi-million dollar broadcasting empire that would stretch across western Canada.

Listeners tuning in to the new radio station were treated to soft sophisticated sounds, spiritual nourishment and a deep commitment to rural life. In those days of cold war uncertainty, the space race, Marilyn Munroe, and the emergence of rock 'n' roll, CFAM was indeed a sea of tranquility in a turbulent world. At least that was the appearance from the outside. Inside, the station was anything but tranquil.

The early days of CFAM were hardly easy. The station had trouble keeping staff. Many potential advertisers were not certain what radio should or could do for them. "Advertisers were afraid of being identified with those 'Mennonite crackpots' who thought they could operate a radio station," declared company President Walter Kroeker, when he spoke

THE ARTIST

According to an old radio adage, a good announcer will paint a word picture so that listeners can visualize what is being talked about. George Balcan possessed that skill, although it was but a portion of his creative genius. Balcan could literally paint a picture that would hold up to critical acclaim. Nineteen-year-old George Adelard Alfred Balcaen (he later dropped the e) was the first announcer hired for the brand new radio station in Dauphin. Born in St. Boniface, Balcan had moved to Dauphin with his parents and worked in the family grocery store. As a teenager, he spent hours listening to American radio that could be easily picked up on cold winter nights. Jazz was his favourite music.

The arrival of CKDM in Dauphin in 1950 offered a new opportunity. Young George made the most of it, using Dauphin as a stepping stone for a broadcasting career that spanned more than 40 years. For the better part of three decades, he was one of the most popular morning men in Montreal, working most of that time at CJAD.

Although a successful broadcaster, his first love was art. Even as a youngster, he was interested in drawing. Art provided a creative outlet that could never be fulfilled as a radio broadcaster. At the time of his death in 2004, The *Globe and Mail* described him as "one of Canada's premier pastel artists." Paintings such as "Danseuse au Repose", "On the Steps" and "Venice Flower Market" have hung in galleries across the country, including the National Art Gallery in Ottawa.

The teenager who launched his career at CKDM Dauphin was named to the Order of Canada in 1998.

to shareholders a few years after the station opened. Hildebrand recalls how some businesses, after initially advertising with CFAM, refused to renew their contracts because there had been no dramatic increase in sales. Within a year of the station's launch, dissension developed within the board of directors. Company President A.J. Thiessen, the man who had worked so hard to get the station up and running, abruptly quit, divesting himself of all interest in the operation. "I really wondered at times if those Altona boys were going to make it," recalled Les Garside years later.

Thiessen not only walked away from CFAM, but within a year had put together a group of investors seeking a licence to establish a radio station in Steinbach. The announcement shook the board of Southern Manitoba Broadcasting. "We fully realize that the establishment of such a station within our listening area would have disastrous consequences for CFAM," company President Walter Kroeker told shareholders. The prospect of a full-scale fight between the Mennonite business elite

was further complicated by the fact one of the Steinbach investors happened to be the father-in-law of CFAM General Manager Dennis Barkman. At the licensing hearing, Southern Manitoba Broadcasting made its case against the new station, and in the end, the Board of Broadcast Governors turned down the proposal for the Steinbach station. By 1964, Southern Manitoba Broadcasting had established its own station in Steinbach, with most of the programming originating in Altona. In the early '70s, a similar station was set up in Boissevain.

The station's music policy was strict. Classical works, light classics, hymns, choirs, traditional old world music and choral works were standard fare. Almost from the beginning, CFAM was the "go-to" station for Christmas music. Yet the early years saw bitter conflict over music. CFAM dubbed itself "the good music station," but the definition of "good music" was open to interpretation. The first music director, Ben Horch, was a gifted musician and conductor with an engrained commitment to classical works. In Ben's world, there was little

tolerance for modern music, much of which he considered un-Christian and anti-culture. Brilliant as he was, Horch could be headstrong and petulant. Suggestions by some board members that the station offer some lighter classics or even western music were met with derision. His biographer, Peter Letkemann, writes of continual clashes between the music director and station management:

"Ben had well-defined opinions of what did and did not constitute good music, and right from the beginning there was a diversity of opinion between Ben and various members of the Board of Directors." Esther (Horch's wife) wrote:

"The Board of Directors who had invested money were out to make money. Ben in turn was out to stimulate interest in music, and since it was coined the good music station he was ready to prove it to be so...as early as March 22, 1957, just a week after broadcasting began, A.J. Thiessen wanted to change Ben's morning symphony to gospel song programs. Ben was furious."

During a tumultuous two years, Horch established high standards that won critical acclaim even though certain on air escapades pushed management to the limit. One particular annoyance, as cited by Letkemann, was a proclivity to "forget" to read commercials during his broadcasts. In 1959, Horch moved on to become a "serious music producer" at CBC Winnipeg. CFAM's music policy remained strict, although perhaps less restrictive than during its first two years. Future music directors such as Leonard Enns and Ray Saunders worked long hours to maintain the station's musical standards. The library was one of the most extensive of any radio station in the country, with over 9,000 recordings. Cuts on long-play recordings were often covered with coloured dots...music that was not permitted over the CFAM airwaves. On some occasions, listeners heard the music but not the full name of the artist. The Mormon Tabernacle Choir, for example, was often played on CFAM. It was always identified as the Tabernacle Choir, as Mormonism was not viewed as a Christian sect.

Flowing directly from the high quality music policy was an advertising issue that presented the station with a perplexing dilemma. By the late 1950s and early '60s, the use of musical jingles and sound effects was common in radio commercials. The music used in these spots tended to be fast-paced, upbeat and, in the view of some, even "jazzy"... in short, at odds with the station's musical standards. National advertisers, however, were making extensive use of radio jingles and CFAM stood to lose significant revenue should it choose not to run such advertising. Company treasurer D.K. Friesen sought out the opinion of shareholders. In a letter to directors he noted that while some listeners had complained, there was also the fact that "musical jingle sponsors will spend $20,000 with us during 1960." At least one shareholder, Ted Friesen, urged his colleagues to stay the course. "I for one would not be willing to compromise for the sake of economic consideration," he wrote. "In defining our musical policy on the other hand, I would not be averse to the use of sound effects in advertising,

IF WE CAN MAKE IT THERE

start

For many an entertainer, receiving critical acclaim in the New York press is the ultimate symbol of success. The odds of a small rural Manitoba radio station being written up by the *New York Times* are almost unfathomable. Yet that is exactly what happened when, in 1961, the *Times* commissioned an article about CFAM radio in Altona, Manitoba. The following is an excerpt from the story which appeared on March 9 of that year.

> "The truth of the matter, however, is that this relatively small broadcasting operation in the Manitoba hinterlands...small certainly, in terms of the bigger and more powerful outlets of the big cities...is by all standards and measurements one of the most interesting and significant radio outlets in all of Canada, if not North America.
>
> It is interesting because, despite the fact that it is located in a farm community where the standards of radio broadcasting are usually attuned to the basic needs of the individual farmer, CFAM has established a sophisticated broadcasting pattern that puts many a big city radio outlet to shame.
>
> It is significant because the commercial success of station CFAM would seem to reflect a growing need for broadcasters to understand the desires of 'grass roots' listeners, as it were, for programming that will satisfy their cultural and spiritual, as well as their practical need."
>
> *Source: New York Times*

such as cackling hens, or other gimmicks as long as they are not objectionable in a common-sensible way nor would all musical jingles in my opinion be classified as such but the ones I have heard are mostly jazzy and conflict with our musical standards." Ultimately, compromise won the day. Many, but not all, jingles were permitted. They were, however, restricted to certain hours of the programming day.

Despite early growing pains, CFAM also had advantages. It was a local business in an area where people liked to keep their money at home. Mennonite communities had embraced credit unions and co-ops for the expressed purpose of developing local business. The station would not accept liquor, cigarette or gambling advertising, nor were any commercials run on Sunday. What CFAM did welcome was religious programming, not just on Sunday, but every day of the week. Such programming provided a steady revenue stream. According to a 1961 director's report, one program known as the "Voice of China and Asia" was netting the station $6,000 a year. Another, "The People's Gospel Hour," was dropped because the producers were slow to pay. One "Back to the Bible" series received 3,000 responses from CFAM listeners. The station had a Religious Advisory Committee which reported that in one year early in the 1960s, 28 religious programs were aired regularly, while 46 churches took part in live broadcasts. With its music and religious programming, the station set itself far apart from other broadcasters.

The programming struck a chord well beyond the region. With the CFAM signal easily heard in Winnipeg, the station also developed a loyal urban following...which also served to provide additional advertising revenue. "We always had a significant audience in Winnipeg and that was because of the music and the general family value tone," says Elmer Hildebrand. "We always managed to have a significant number of advertisers in Winnipeg."

The early success sparked what turned out to be a bad business decision. Southern Manitoba Broadcasting applied and received approval for an FM classical music radio station. Studios were located in St. Norbert. In retrospect, it could be argued the Altona broadcasters were ahead of their time, as FM radio would later emerge as a preferred listening source. But in 1962, FM was in its infancy. The fact that most home radios didn't have FM was a major problem. Southern Manitoba Broadcasting went so far as to try to sell FM receivers in retail outlets below the going price. The plan represented a complete reversal of history. Early radio stations were started to try to sell radios. Now radios were being sold to try to sell the station. It didn't work. With the FM operation losing money, it was sold in 1965 to the Canadian Broadcasting Corporation, becoming CBC FM and eventually CBC Radio Two.

With the Pembina Valley region laying claim to some of the highest quality farm land in the province, CFAM committed considerable resources to agricultural coverage. Dr. Peter Olson was the first farm director, later followed by Bruce Gunn and Bob Paschke. An early-morning farm broadcast, a noon agricultural program and market updates throughout the day were all part of the service. There was particular emphasis on special crops grown in the region, such as sugar beets and sunflowers. Each day, after the two o'clock news, an announcer would slowly and methodically read a long list of closing grain prices. While less than compelling radio, it did provide a vital service. Elevator agents had time to write the prices down and set the amount farmers would receive for that day's deliveries.

Programming for children was another of the station's popular features. Esther Horch (Tanta Esther) provided the first broadcasts for youngsters. Aunt Olly (Penner) followed and an entire generation of children looked for their birthday presents "behind the couch" or "in the refrigerator," depending on the directions provided over the radio. Saturday mornings, children could listen to the adventures of a young Christian teen named Danny Orlis.

Elmer Hildebrand worked his way up the ranks, moving from copywriter to sales representative. There was no denying his keen business acumen. By the early 1960s, he had obtained shares in the company. In 1967, he was named general manager. Hildebrand's philosophy could be summed up in a single word...local. He stressed coverage of community events and local happenings. Fed up with a large turnover in staff during his early years, he implemented a policy of hiring people from the region and training them as broadcasters. It was his hope that people who saw southern Manitoba as home would be more inclined to build a career at the station. To a significant degree, the policy worked. Numerous local residents spent their entire careers at the station, including newsman Harv Kroeker from Winkler, receptionist Dorothy Klassen of Altona, creative writer Cleo Heinrichs from Plum Coulee and sales representative David Wiebe of Altona, who eventually took over as general manager of CFAM.

Ironically, an exception Hildebrand made to his own rule turned out to be one of the most shrewd human resource decisions ever made at the station. In 1965, Hildebrand, Walter Kroeker and D.K. Friesen travelled to Winnipeg for a meeting with a service station operator on Pembina Highway...a former CKRC broadcaster who had recently left the business. CFAM was in need of a morning man and the garage owner was being considered for the job.

Jim McSweeny was a gregarious Irishman who had been born and raised in Winnipeg, cut his broadcasting teeth in Dauphin, moved to CKRC in Winnipeg and then abandoned radio to operate an Esso service station. He could spin a yarn that would make his Mennonite suitors cringe, but he was also a real broadcaster who understood what it took to attract and hold an audience.

Although experienced, McSweeny was hardly an obvious choice. He knew little about the Mennonite way of life, was not particularly religious, and at previous radio stations, his stock in trade had been pop and country music. Admittedly, it was a difficult transition. "I was ready to quit after the first month...there was so much you couldn't play or couldn't say."

Yet stay he did, and over the next 30 years "the Morning Minstrel," as his show was called, captured the hearts of his southern Manitoba listeners. The name McSweeny became synonymous with CFAM. His down home humour and constant name dropping had widespread appeal. If John and Mary Epp had met him at an event the night before, they would be sure to hear their names on the radio the next morning. Countless public appearances had him on a first name basis with many of his listeners. Working his craft, local names such as Gnadenthal and Schoenwiese flowed from his lips as though he had lived in the region his entire life. His presence at a car dealership, furniture store, fair or festival was certain to attract a crowd. "I can't remember many days when that (morning) show was not sold out," recalls McSweeny.

One other feature of Jim McSweeny's morning show was not only unique, but attracted a loyal audience like no other. Every morning just after the nine o'clock news, Jim read the funeral announcements. Undertakers, or in some cases individuals, would provide information on the latest deaths, including time and whereabouts of the funeral. It was no public service. There was a charge for each announcement. For some listeners, it was a feature never to be missed. In slow somber tones, McSweeny would perform. He could make any obituary sound like the passing of his best friend.

On any given day there could be ten or more. "Sometimes I'd still be going at a quarter after nine," McSweeny remembers. Long after McSweeny's departure, the funeral announcements remained a fixture at the radio station.

The combination of a popular morning show, local information, a unique music policy and religious broadcasting turned CFAM into a lucrative operation. Over time, Elmer Hildebrand took over ownership of the company. From the base in Altona, Southern Manitoba Broadcasting undertook an aggressive expansion policy, purchasing or establishing stations in mostly small and medium-sized markets across the country, particularly on the prairies. The formula was always the same: hire local broadcasters to provide local service. Hildebrand became an influential force in numerous local and national broadcast organizations. The company's name was changed to Golden West Broadcasting. By 2012, Golden West operated a network of 40 radio stations in Manitoba, Saskatchewan and Alberta. The little station for Mennonites had become a broadcasting empire.

"From my perspective," says Hildebrand, "the two most important things in our company that we ever did was hire locally and do all local news...that makes us relevant." In 2012, Elmer Hildebrand was named to the Order of Canada for his work in developing community service radio.

CHAPTER EIGHT

Farmin' and Learnin'

Throughout the 1950s, agriculture remained a mainstay of the Manitoba economy. The number of people living on farms or in small communities outnumbered those living in Winnipeg. Politicians from the countryside wielded significant influence as the majority of representatives in the Manitoba Legislature came from rural areas. As the centre of the grain trade, Winnipeg was still very much a farm town.

From the beginning, agriculture was a key component of radio programming. CKY had barely begun broadcasting when it was caught in the middle of a growing controversy over grain marketing. In the wake of a collapse in wheat prices after the First World War, the Grain Exchange and the newly formed farmer-run wheat pools were at war. One of CKY's early sponsors was a publication called the *Grain Trade News*, owned by Dawson Richardson, an Exchange member. The publication paid $35 a month for a daily 15-minute program which provided closing markets and grain trade news. Another feature was a regular commentary, written by Sanford Evans (the same man who had listened to Lee De Forest's very first radio broadcast in Winnipeg). As editor of the *Grain News*, Evans espoused the "glories" of the Grain Exchange, while condemning the wheat pools at every opportunity.

Not to be outdone, the pools bought their own radio time immediately following the *Grain News* program and proceeded to raise the rhetoric with daily tirades against the Exchange. According to one account provided by radio pioneer and historian Austin Weir, Premier Bracken stepped in, demanding CKY drop the Exchange programming. MTS Commissioner John Lowry, who was responsible for CKY, balked at the idea and instead asked listeners if they wanted the grain prices continued. The vast majority of respondents said "yes" and the broadcasts continued, although the editorials from both sides were cut.

Opposite: Lionel Moore broadcasting from Brandon Winter Fair. S.J MCKEE ARCHIVES, BRANDON UNIVERSITY

Over the years, there were many practical ways in which radio assisted farmers, not the least of which was helping locate stray animals. In July of 1938, the magazine *Manitoba Calling* published an article about the large number of requests CKX and CKY were receiving about lost farm animals. In one documented case, "CKX in co-operation with the RCMP broadcast a description of two horses alleged to have been stolen. Twenty minutes after the announcement went on the air, the Mounted Police made an arrest some 50 miles from Brandon, this result being directly attributable to the Brandon station's contact with a wide audience."

The farm broadcast

Many broadcasting careers have had some strange beginnings, but none quite so unusual as that of Lionel Moore Senior. Moore, whose voice was synonymous with farm broadcasting in Manitoba for more than three decades, literally kicked off his career by being kicked...by a cow. Moore was standing on the edge of a truck applying a liquid brand to a newborn calf. The protective mother applied a well-placed kick, sending the future broadcaster flying. "I can still see that old black cow," recalled Moore in an interview more than 30 years after the injury. "She didn't like me very much." While in hospital recovering from his injuries, Moore saw a newspaper advertisement from Inland Broadcasting. The programming and production company was looking for someone to collect and broadcast farm market prices. Having worked as a cattle buyer at St. Boniface stock yards, Moore was familiar with stock quotes, but was admittedly less than skilled as a broadcaster. Upon being hired, his first task was to provide a market report to the radio station in Yorkton. "I was very fortunate nobody in Manitoba could hear me blundering through those early market broadcasts."

Through his job at Inland, Moore crossed paths with CBC farm broadcasters Bob Knowles (a future United Nations representative with the Food and Agriculture Organization) and Peter Whittall (who would go on to become television's Mr. Fix-it). In 1950, he made the move to the Corporation.

The CBC "Farm Broadcast" was more than just a radio program. With its market reports, weather forecasts, crop outlooks, husbandry advice and farm news, the program was in fact an important ingredient in determining the decisions farmers made as to what crops to plant or when to sell their livestock and produce. "Half a million dollars worth of cattle are sold in the heavy fall marketing season on the basis of CBC market reports," declared the in-house publication *CBC Times* in an early 1950s article. "Lionel Moore has seen many a shrewd buyer's deal queered when 'The Farm Broadcast' came on during the lunch hour with reports of higher prices."

Moore himself could provide a specific example. He liked to tell the story of a feedlot operator from Warren named Royden Riddell. "We met at Brandon Fair and he told me 'just two weeks ago I was on my way in (to market) with three truckloads of cattle from the feedlot and I heard you giving the market report. I stopped those trucks and turned them around and took them back home.' That," said Moore, "made me realize the importance of the information we put on the farm broadcast."

In addition to in-studio work, Moore travelled the Prairies extensively, searching out the stories of the farm community. By his own estimates, during one two-week period in June 1952, he and a CBC technician travelled 2,000 miles throughout northeastern Saskatchewan and northwestern Manitoba. "The Farm Broadcast" from the Royal Winter Fair in Brandon became an institution. From heavy horses to stock sales, the CBC Farm Broadcast was there. On one occasion, Moore even presided over a square dancing competition. When the day was finally over, broadcasters, farmers and others connected to agriculture would gather, most often in Moore's hotel room "for food and a few drinks." In the future, the practice would become known as networking.

A radio soap opera known as "The Jacksons" developed a large and loyal following on "The Farm Broadcast," not just in rural areas but also in Winnipeg. Saskatoon author Mary Rogers Pattison wrote the daily feature about a farm family in the fictitious community of Little Coulee that could have been just about anywhere on the Prairies. It was the story of "Dollar Dick Jackson" who loved auction sales, his daughter Colleen, son Buddy, and their neighbours. The storylines were real and easily identifiable, and could be based on nothing more than a faulty machinery part or a winter carnival. The actors and actresses changed over the years and included Ed McCrea, Colleen Davis and Margaret Brown. According to the CBC, "The Jacksons" was meant to be much more than just noon hour fluff. "The goal was to impart useful information about the latest farming methods and issues in an informal and easily digested way," declared a *CBC Times* article in 1952. "Dollar Dick and his neighbours are no laggards when it comes to agriculture, and they let drop a hint now and then which may solve many a difficulty for the prairie farmer."

CANADIAN BROADCASTING CORPORATION

School Broadcasts 1958-59

CBC School Broadcast Study Guide.
ANDREW MOIR, GARRY MOIR COLLECTION

"People would come (to the studio) every day to see 'The Farm Broadcast' and 'The Jacksons,'" remembered Moore. "Sometimes a dozen...some days 100." A note from a listener in Orkney, Saskatchewan perhaps best summed up "The Jacksons" appeal. "They are so darn natural it's like our own community."

Throughout the 1940s and '50s, Farm Radio Forums were popular across rural Canada. The unique programming concept involved the CBC farm broadcasters, the Canadian Federation of Agriculture and the Canadian Association for Adult Education. Every Monday night during the fall and winter, groups of farmers would gather, usually in someone's home, to listen to a radio broadcast focussing on some rural issue. Topics varied significantly and included debates on "Farming as a Career," "The Role of Women in Public Life," and "The Mechanization of Our Farms." When the broadcast ended, the small groups would enter into their own discussions. A group leader would record what the farmers were saying and pass the information back to the Farm Radio Forum. In addition to educating and contributing to the development of agricultural policy, the forums also played an important social function. They provided an opportunity for farming neighbours to get together and talk about mutual problems. In some instances, the groups also served as welcoming committees for new immigrant families that had arrived in the community. "The Forum has brought back to the community a warmth of friendly feeling that had almost completely disappeared," wrote Dr. E.A. Corbett, the first executive director of The Canadian Association for Adult Education. In Manitoba, the popularity of the Farm Forums reached a peak in 1949-50 when 116 farmer groups were registered. So successful was the concept that several other nations such as India, Ghana and France set up their own Forums.

Over time, programming to the farm community became an exercise in catering to a shrinking audience. The total number of Manitoba farms peaked in the early 1940s at 58,000. What followed was a steady and continuous decline that would alter the social fabric of rural life. To survive in a fiercely competitive world market, farmers found it necessary to increase the size of their operations. Larger, technologically-advanced agricultural equipment, fertilizers and chemicals helped boost productivity but also resulted in skyrocketing costs. In the name of efficiency, the railroads abandoned thousands of miles of rail lines. Grain elevators in many a small town shut down. Schools consolidated, resulting in another blow to smaller communities. Thousands of rural residents, a great many of them young people, headed to urban centres to find work. According to the 2006 census, Manitoba had just over 19,000 farms.

Each of these developments had a significant impact on the way radio stations and farm broadcasters went about their business. Chronicling such dramatic change and adapting to ever-shifting demographics was no small feat.

In 1966, an affable 25-year-old from Calgary named Jim Rae joined the CBC farm crew. He had actually tried to land

MIRACLE AT MALTON

October 3, 1959 was a rainy Saturday night. Lionel Moore was far from the Prairies he knew so well. Returning from a farm broadcasters' conference, Moore was sitting on a Trans Canada Airlines Viscount aircraft en route from Montreal to Winnipeg via Toronto. Storms had developed over the Toronto area as the aircraft made its approach to the airport in Malton. Seatbelts were secured as the turbo-prop nosed downward. Then in Moore's words "we did touch down with a terrific thud, then smooth, then a series of thuds, then kind of a grinding sensation like driving a car with four flat tires. Then apparently we hit a wire fence and the plane bucked and turned and we were treated to a ride just as I imagine it must be like in one of those chuck wagons at the Calgary Stampede." The aircraft had landed 400 feet short of the runway. The plane was all but demolished as seats were torn loose and the floor and roof of the fuselage broke open.

Toronto newspapers called it the "Miracle at Malton." The plane had narrowly missed a hydro transformer which experts claimed later would almost certainly have exploded, engulfing the aircraft in flames. Of the 39 passengers on board, four were injured, including two CBC farm broadcast employees from Toronto. Future "Hockey Night in Canada" host Ward Cornell was also on the plane. No one was killed. Moore walked away with only a bruise to his mid-section. He returned to Winnipeg the next day and was back at work Monday preparing "The Farm Broadcast."

In recounting the experience to CBC listeners, Moore left out one important detail. Also on the aircraft that night was a Nova Scotia mother and her seven-month old twin daughters. She was travelling to Winnipeg to visit her husband who was with the RCAF. When the plane hit the ground, one of the babies was thrown from her arms and ended up under a seat. In the darkness that rainy night, the mother screamed for her child. Lionel Moore scooped up both babies and handed them to safety out the aircraft window.

start here ↓

a job at the corporation two years earlier, but Lionel Moore concluded the youngster did not have the proper experience. Rae's parents had operated a dairy farm and later a cow-calf operation near Calgary. As a boy, Jim was active in 4H, raising and showing pure bred steers and heifers. In high school came a hint of his future career when he was named public speaking champion in a competition run by the United Church in Calgary. After garnering a degree in Agriculture, he went to work at Federated Co-op, all the while sending his resume to local radio stations.

On his arrival at CBC Winnipeg, Rae quickly discovered that radio and farm broadcasting would require a demanding learning curve. One of his early tasks was reading fish prices. "Lionel Moore rode my ass continually," recalled Rae. "After every show I was called in and he'd go over my scripts and (voice) inflection." The advice was obviously well-taken as Rae would succeed Moore as the voice of agriculture in Manitoba. Like his predecessors, Rae travelled the length and breadth of the province.

"I don't believe there's a small community I haven't been to." In his 30-year career, he missed the Royal Winter Fair in Brandon only once. "We were a big part of their fair... they considered us to be really important."

On one occasion, Rae was sent to Rome for a Conference of the United Nations Food and Agriculture Organization, and for a number of years he attended the annual farm outlook conference in Washington DC, sponsored by the United States Department of Agriculture. As a farm journalist, Rae's contact list was second to none.

Rae reported extensively on the Hall Commission on rail line abandonment, the demise of the St. Boniface stock yards, and was on hand when Ottawa eliminated the Crows Nest Pass grain freight rate. Each of these events had a significant impact on rural life.

The CBC Farm and Fish department was eventually phased out with agriculture falling under the purview of current events programming. "Radio Noon," as it came to be called, consisted of a producer and two farm co-hosts. Rae's partners

included Dennis Sherbanick, Jim Feeny and Diane Wreford. Veteran farm broadcaster George Price, who had previously worked in Winnipeg, provided coverage and commentaries from Ottawa. Consumer commentators were brought in to appeal to a growing urban population. Market reports were scaled back. As programming evolved, stories about other resources, environmental issues, nutrition and animal rights became part of the mix. Radio was no longer simply programming information to and for farmers. It was also telling their story to an audience often far removed from the wheat field or the feedlot.

Young Manitoba Listens

Next to the grain elevator, the one-room school best symbolized rural life on the Prairies. The tiny schools dotted the Manitoba landscape from before the 1920s into the 1960s. Here again, Manitoba broadcasters broke new ground by utilizing radio as an educational tool.

CKY's first manager, D.R.P Coats, maintained a strongly held belief that education was a primary function of the new medium. One of his first programming decisions was to convince the University of Manitoba to have professors offer lectures over the airwaves. This was a Canadian first and lasted for more than two decades. Dr. William Talbot Allison, a Presbyterian minister and English professor, became a well-known radio personality. He began lecturing and offering book reviews in 1923 and continued on CKY for more than 15 years.

For young children, Coats doubled as "Uncle Peter," whose stories always contained a dose of informational material, particularly in the area of science. Uncle Peter would talk about everything from water safety to astronomy to aerodynamics (kite flying). When the opportunity presented itself, Brandon's "Bird Lady" would be brought on the program. The Bird Lady, a Ms. C. I. Todd, had her own nature program on CKX in which she waxed eloquent about the vast array of birds in Manitoba.

She even had her own club known as the O-Pee-Chee Club. According to one account in *Manitoba Calling*, "her Saturday morning talks are proving tremendously popular with young folks and old folks too." The article went on to note that when Ms. Todd visited Turtle Plains School in western Manitoba "she found all the pupils were members of the O-Pee-Chee Club."

As early as 1925, the Manitoba Teachers Federation took it upon itself to produce school programming, which was another Canadian first. By the 1930s, the provincial Department of Education had become involved, as had the Canadian Broadcasting Corporation. CKY made available two half-hour time slots each week for educational programs. Despite the well-meaning efforts of all involved, economic conditions in the '30s severely limited what could be accomplished. It was quickly discovered that most schools, particularly in rural Manitoba, couldn't afford the cost of a radio.

Not until near the end of the Second World War did school broadcasting really take hold in Manitoba, thanks in part to a

young woman who would become one of the best-known educational broadcasters in the world.

Gertrude McCance was born and raised in St. James. After receiving a degree from the University of Manitoba, she went to England to study speech training. Following a brief stint as a teacher in Toronto, McCance returned to Manitoba where, in 1944, she was appointed Director of School Broadcasts for the Department of Education. The school broadcasts were a joint effort between the CBC and the provincial government. The CBC supplied studio time and technical support, while the Education Department provided the creative component.

McCance brought endless energy and enthusiasm to her work. Not only was she instrumental in developing unique educational programs, she performed on them as well. A newspaper article once described her as "the best known woman to Manitoba school children." In addition to the regular broadcasts, she and other Department of Education staff produced a manual sent out to all teachers

Gertrude McCance : Young Manitoba Listens Magazine. ANDREW MOIR. GARRY MOIR COLLECTION

GERTRUDE F. McCANCE
Supervisor of School Broadcasts,
Manitoba Dept. of Education

entitled *Young Manitoba Listens*. It served as a guide to each program and offered advice to teachers on how to make the most effective use of the school broadcast. Although small in stature (McCance was barely five feet tall), she could be demanding. Certainly more than one CBC producer experienced the "wrath of Gertrude." One contemporary described her as "a mighty mite who can get anything done."

With few exceptions, the School Broadcasts ran Monday through Friday from 3:00 to 3:30. No doubt for some pupils the program was looked forward to with great enthusiasm, as it meant the day was near an end. On Fridays, the CBC network provided its own program; the rest of the week was the responsibility of the Department of Education. A program called "Let's Sing Together" was an early hit. Another favourite was titled "Adventures in Speech," in which McCance would exhort her young audience to speak proper and eloquent English. It was an exercise in interactive radio, as students were urged to try techniques exercising the tongue, the

lips and the jaw. Most fun were the tongue-twisters McCance utilized, such as "she says she will sew a sheet."

"It's Fun to Draw" was probably the least likely and most successful of all the school broadcasts. Using drama, music, stories and poetry, students were urged to let their creativity flow and draw what they were hearing. "After each broadcast," notes historian Richard Lambert, "hundreds of pictures began to pour into McCance's office." Eventually, the best drawings would be used as the cover of the publication *Young Manitoba Listens*, which was distributed to schools across Manitoba. "Pictures come from all over the province," wrote McCance in one educational publication, "not just the big schools with skilled art teachers but from one-room rural schools and from areas so remote that pupils would rarely, if ever, have access to an art gallery or a display of adult painting."

"It's Fun to Draw" became a model for school programs in other provinces and was written up in *Saturday Night* magazine. The true measure of the program's success came from a broadcast leading up to the coronation of Queen Elizabeth in 1953. It described in vivid terms the city of London leading up to the event. As a result of the broadcast, some 5,000 drawings were mailed in to the office of the School Broadcasts.

The Department of Education pushed radio in the schools. There are many stories of department inspectors making sure teachers were using the medium. According to one account, an inspector arrived at a one-room school only to discover there was no radio. To ensure the pupils heard the broadcast that day, the inspector opened a school window, pulled his vehicle close to the building and turned up the volume on the car radio.

The Manitoba School Broadcasts won numerous national and international awards. Gertrude McCance was a much sought after speaker at educational conferences across Canada and the United States. "Americans in educational broadcasting have much to learn from Gertrude McCance," declared the *St. Louis Post Dispatch*, in a 1957 article. In 1961, she was called to South Africa to talk about the program. Educational radio in Manitoba had truly become a model for the rest of the world.

At its peak, it is estimated the School Broadcasts had a captive audience of 180,000 students.

Yet, not everyone was being forced to listen. As early as 1945, *Manitoba Calling* noted that "the quality of Canadian school broadcasts is such that they now claim a wide audience outside the school."

Gertrude McCance could attest to that. One letter she received, after a broadcast featuring poetry, came from a prisoner at a local jail. "As I will be spending some time in this gaol, I would like to know what you think of my talents for writing poetry." The man had sent along a number of handwritten poems . McCance immediately thought the poetry seemed familiar and upon further research found that the poems had been pilfered from a recent magazine.

The decline in rural population, school mergers, television and eventually digital technology would bring an end to school radio broadcasting. By 1980, the CBC wanted out of the business of education because of rising production costs and a dwindling student audience. The fact that the Corporation had moved the time of the broadcasts to two in the afternoon didn't help. That just happened to coincide with recess at most schools. "The school broadcasts have been a marvellous institution," declared Neil Harris, the final supervisor of school broadcasting for the Department of Education, "but times have changed."

CHAPTER NINE

Fab Fifties

The last weekend of September 1953 was crisp and bright as thousands of Winnipeggers stood on Portage Avenue waiting to tour brand new CBC radio facilities. The building, which had earlier housed a garage and automobile dealership, looked nothing like it had previously. Purchased from James Richardson and Company for $260,000, the CBC had spent another $1.2 million completely gutting the structure and turning it into a state of the art broadcast centre.

Located north of Portage between Young and Spence, the renovated three-storey building housed seven radio studios, a library, newsroom, technical facilities and administrative offices for the entire CBC prairie region. A semi-spiral staircase greeted those who entered the front door. The stairway led to a mezzanine floor which was the nerve centre for radio in Manitoba, Saskatchewan and northwestern Ontario. Six thousand square feet near the rear of the main floor had been set aside for a new medium known as television.

On the evening of May 31, 1954, the Georgian Room on the fifth floor of the Hudson's Bay department store was buzzing with excitement. Winnipeg's first television station, CBWT, was about to go on the air. The always exquisite restaurant had been transformed into a large display centre with television sets scattered throughout the room. Customers had been invited to the Georgian Room to witness history being made only a few blocks away. Some of the screens were snowy, while others had wavy lines. The first image seen was a test pattern...a large circle that looked something like a dartboard with a sketch of an Indian chief in full headdress. After the test pattern, up popped a still photograph of the Queen.

Back at the CBC building, veteran radio man Maurice Burchell watched all the activity with some trepidation. His voice had been the first heard on CBC Manitoba when CBW took over from CKY. Now he

Opposite: Santa on the radio was a Christmas tradition.
CKSB COLLECTION: LA SOCIETE HISTORIQUE DE SAINT BONIFACE

start here
↓

had been assigned to read the first television newscast. Whatever nervousness Burchell may have felt was apparently not evident as he faced the camera that opening night. "A good appearance, voice and personality puts Burchell on par with the best US television has to offer in the way of news broadcasters," gushed the *Tribune*'s Ann Henry in a review of the CBC's first telecast. Television had arrived in Winnipeg.

At the very beginning, television's impact on radio was relatively small. Virtually every household claimed one or two radio receivers. The automobile radio, while not necessarily a standard feature, was easily obtained by any motorist who wanted one. By contrast, television sets were expensive, with owners requiring an aerial on top of their home. Snowy screens, wavy lines and rolling images were common. And television's hours were limited; CBWT did not go on the air until late in the afternoon and signed off shortly after 11pm.

Radio was, by now, a mature medium with local stations competing fiercely for listeners and advertising dollars.

Programming was aimed at the widest possible audience, with most private broadcasters keeping a close eye on production costs. Commercial radio's emphasis on programming to a "lowbrow" audience would come in for criticism throughout the decade.

As television viewing grew in the evening, the radio morning show became increasingly important. It was the era of the big voice and fun-filled mornings. Many of Winnipeg's legendary personalities came into their own in the 1950s...among them, Cliff Gardner, who hosted the CJOB morning show from 1949 to '56 before being lured away by CKRC. The job at CKRC came open with the departure of one of Winnipeg's most popular morning men, Bill Walker. Political correctness had not yet permeated the local vernacular as "Big Chief" Walker left his "Wigwam" at CKRC, moving to Toronto and national television fame.

Gardner was the consummate professional and would become a Winnipeg institution, not only in broadcasting but also in theatre. Born in Brandon, he began

his career at age 16 at CKX. Moving to Winnipeg five years later, Gardner may have had the broadest range of talent of any broadcaster in the country. Former colleague John Cochrane recalls him doing a "bright and funny" morning show. Shortly after the show he would record a program that ran late in the evening which would sound positively dreamy. "He was the ultimate pro," says Cochrane. "He could do a voice track or commercial or promo in any style you wanted. He was maybe the best radio guy I've ever seen in terms of on the air."

Former CKRC staffer Jim McSweeny remembers Gardner's passion as a performer. "Cliff really wanted to be an actor," says McSweeny. Indeed, as early as 1953, Gardner was on stage with the Winnipeg Little Theatre company and would make a name for himself in numerous Rainbow Stage productions. Gardner took his work seriously and was always demanding of himself; on occasion he could be overly sensitive to criticism. "If he got one (critical) phone call when he was doing his morning

CKRC Morning man Cliff Gardner.
GARDNER FAMILY

show," says Cochrane, "he'd be done for the day. It would really throw him. He was just so intense." One of Gardner's creative specialities was adapting popular songs with local lyrics. His best-known effort came in 1958 during the lead up to the Grey Cup game between the Winnipeg Blue Bombers and the arch-rival Hamilton Tiger Cats. A hit of the day told the story of the unfortunate Tom Dooley, a man about to be hanged. Gardner modified the lyrics to fit the mood of the 1950s Blue Bomber crowd:

"Hang down your head Jim Trimble
(the Tiger Cats coach),
Hang down your head and cry.
You said you'd beat the Bombers.
Now eat your humble pie.
The 29th of November,
reckon where you will be...
down in the lonesome locker,
Crying in misery."

This little ditty proved so popular it was recorded and sold, with the money going to a local charity.

At both CKRC and CJOB, Gardner was the football club's biggest booster, eventually being named to the Bomber's Hall of Fame. In a career that spanned over 60 years, he was also one of the city's biggest boosters. He had the opportunity to leave several times for larger markets but always chose to stay. Eventually he returned to CJOB as program director. Sons Greg and Ford followed their father, also working in Winnipeg radio.

Cliff Gardner's departure to CKRC in 1956 left CJOB with a huge hole to fill. The station was far from the dominant force it would become and needed to keep pace with its competitors. The new morning man would be a 29-year-old carrot-top who had spent his formative years on the family farm in Bladworth, Saskatchewan. John Joseph Alix, better known as " Red," loved to sing. His first job in radio was crooning country ballads at a station in Saskatoon. Alix pioneered a morning segment on CJOB known as "Beefs and Bouquets," one of the very early attempts at interactive radio and a precursor to the radio talk show. As long as

it wasn't libelous, listeners could complain about whatever they wished. Conversely, if they had good news they could hand out a "bouquet." Alix served as CJOB's morning man for 35 years. "Beefs and Bouquets" lasted until Alix retired in the late 1990s, and was resurrected by CJOB on the Hal Anderson morning show in 2012.

Meanwhile, at CKY, a young broadcaster named Eugene Charbonneau was also making his presence felt. To his audience he was simply known as "Porky." A pudgy, happy-go-lucky lad with a signature brush cut and thick glasses, Charbonneau was a country music aficionado . "He was not a cultured radio voice...he was just Porky," says fellow CKY staffer Don Kirton. "And when he got on (the air) people loved him." Charbonneau travelled endless miles around the province, serving as master of ceremonies for country music shows. One country band that appeared regularly on CKY went so far as to call itself the "Porkypiners".

"CKY had to struggle desperately to gain an audience," writes Patrick McDougal, an

original member of the CKY staff. "Porky put CKY in the running."

When CKY began to shift from country to pop music, Porky moved on to Regina. He was replaced by Jack Wells...a big name in Winnipeg radio, but not necessarily a morning man. "Jack didn't really know what to do," says Kirton. The solution was a two-person morning show known as "Cactus Jack's Rumpus Room" with Wells and Kirton. Don Kirton already had considerable morning show experience and could guide Wells through the program. "I would hold up a paper with the temperature," jokes Kirton, "and Jack would read it." In straight-laced '50s radio, where much comedy material came from a joke book, Wells and Kirton were not beyond pushing the envelope. Case in point, the "Dear John Letter" segment where Wells would offer "advice" to the lovelorn. In deep and somber tones, Kirton would read the introduction:

Kirton: And now, time for our Dear John Letter. This morning, a letter from S.J.

Dear John, last night my daughter went out with a new man. When she came home she was wearing a mink coat. Did she do wrong?

Wells: Dear S.J. Well, your daughter may have done wrong, but she didn't do bad. (Chuckle, chuckle, chuckle).

House bands

CKY and CKRC both offered live music with their own "house bands." The CKY Playboys would appear every weekday morning at 6:00. The musicians had to be set up by 5:45. Often the broadcast was the conclusion of an all-nighter as the musicians had never gone to bed after a gig in the countryside the night before. "We never got paid," says Owen Clark, a member of the Playboys. "The exposure, however, was the key for the band to get work. 'If you want the Playboys for your next dance, contact us through CKY'...every time we did a broadcast there would be a slew of letters from rural Manitoba, Saskatchewan or Ontario."

A second well-known group was called the CKY Caravan. It consisted of a family from Auburn, Maine. Performing under the names Hal Lone Pine, Betty Cody and Lone Pine Junior, the CKY country music Caravan developed a large following across the prairies and into the US mid-west. Their real names were Hal and Betty Breau and son Lenny. A genius on the guitar, Lenny Breau would become a music legend. Other local artists touring and performing with the Caravan would also go on to make names for themselves in the world of music...among them Ray St. Germain who was still performing well into his 70s.

The Breaus' decision to move west was of no small significance for CKY. Lone Pine and his family were already successful artists along the eastern seaboard. Two of the station's other popular country performers, Ray and Anne Little, were moving west to Alberta. According to music journalist Ron Forbes Roberts, it was Little who encouraged Breau to move to Winnipeg.

NICKNAMES

During the 1950s and '60s, the radio nickname was very much in vogue. Announcers apparently felt it helped define their on-air persona, or simply fit with the programs they were doing.

Some examples:

"Wild Willy" Grogan

"Cactus" Jack Wells

"Porky" Charbonneau

"Red" Alix

"Suet" Sam

"Hank" McCloy

"Big Chief" Bill Walker

"P.J. the DJ"

"Rowdy Dud" Patterson,
   "howling from 12 to 2, but never blue"

Ron "Keg" Legge

Dennis "Deno" Corrie

"Doc" Steen

"Kay Wise"

Ken "Friar" Nicolson

CKY's Suet Sam (Don Kirton).
WINNIPEG PRESS CLUB COLLECTION.

The first CKY Caravan program aired at 4:00 pm on January 6, 1958. As with the CKY Players, the 15-minute radio program was a means of getting work in small towns across Manitoba, Saskatchewan and North Dakota. Often they would leave a radio station as soon as the program was over, drive for several hours, set up equipment, do the show and arrive back home at two o'clock in the morning. The following day, they would do it all over again.

It was hardly an easy life, and, not surprisingly, the CKY Caravan was relatively short-lived. The family was splitting apart. Lone Pine was known for his quick temper, and on at least one occasion struck his son after a show. Then wife Betty was suddenly dumped from the band. Journalist Forbes Roberts offered this account of the events as they unfolded:

> "Pine decided that the family could no longer
> afford a nanny to look after their children
> and ordered Betty to stay at home with their
> sons when the band was travelling. Betty was
> stunned, but complied with her husband's

wishes. Soon after she discovered Pine's edict was motivated by his affair with 19-year-old Jeannie Ward, one half of the singing sisters act Pine had hired just before firing Betty. Still reeling from this discovery, she learned from the Breaus' landlord that Pine had not paid the rent on their house for several months."

One can only imagine what CKY management was thinking as they witnessed the band carrying the station's name imploding before their eyes. The CKY Caravan contract was not renewed.

The Transistor

On a summer day in 1955, a chance meeting in Tokyo, Japan would have a profound impact on the local radio industry. Winnipeg entrepreneur Albert Cohen was touring Japan as part of a belated honeymoon. Leafing through an English language newspaper, an advertisement caught his attention. A start-up Japanese company was seeking distributors for a new product known as the transistor radio. Cohen set up a meeting with Akio Morita, a co-founder of the Tokyo firm. Intrigued by the tiny radios, Cohen immediately ordered 50 to be sent to Winnipeg. The Japanese company would come to be known as Sony Corporation and Albert Cohen would be its first overseas distributor.

The transistor was an immediate hit, embraced by high school students and young adults. Suddenly, radio was mobile. Radios were heard at parks, beaches, sporting events ... anywhere young people hung out. The impact the transistor had on pop music is incalculable. A PBS documentary summed it up most efficiently. "Teenagers could suddenly listen to music anywhere they wanted, far away from adult ears...it sparked a musical revolution—rock 'n' roll."

"Late night radio listening with a transistor under your pillow was part of the experience for so many of us," says Winnipegger Warren Cosford, who would go on to become one of the nation's top radio producers at CHUM Toronto.

New Regulator

Throughout the 1930s and '40s, radio had developed along two parallel lines...public and private. Certainly that had not been the plan. Officially, Canada had a single broadcasting system as represented by the CBC. The role of private broadcasters was to fill in the gaps left by public radio. The reality was much different. By the 1950s, the two sides were at each other's throats.

Much of the friction stemmed from CBC regulatory control over private radio stations. Anyone establishing a new station had to go to the CBC board of governors for approval. There were restrictions on what type of advertising could be done on radio, and when. Radio broadcasters won a small victory in 1953 when the government decided to drop the $2.50 licence fee required from anyone who owned a radio receiver. In the mid '50s, the CBC launched a probe into whether broadcasters were "buying listeners" with contests and giveaways. Perhaps the most galling for private radio operators was the fact that they had

to compete for advertising dollars with the government-subsidized public broadcaster.

The rhetoric was heated. Critics accused private broadcasters of investing little in programming other than offering popular recordings or sports to attract the widest possible audience for their advertisers. "With a few exceptions, private radio has done nothing" (to support culture), griped University of Manitoba English professor Chester Duncan, who also happened to be a regular commentator on CBC radio. "Sport is the only culture private radio is interested in."

The CBC, in turn, was painted as a bloated, out of touch bureaucracy with programming that ranged from boring to blasphemous. By 1958, the Corporation was running a $1.3 million deficit. A program offering advice on birth control touched off a firestorm of criticism across the nation. In the House of Commons, the Social Credit party suggested the CBC had been infiltrated by Communists.

As in most cases, the true picture lay somewhere in the middle. Private broadcasters certainly were cutting corners to maximize profits, but they were, at the same time, still promoting local musicians, amateur sports teams and a host of other community services. The 1950 flood had clearly demonstrated that broadcasters, both private and public, were ready to step to the plate in a time of crisis.

For its part, the CBC was offering quality programs such as radio drama, classical music and in-depth discussions that were not available anywhere else in the country.

"A separate regulatory body is all that is asked," offered Jack Blick, attempting to strike a conciliatory tone. "I have no quarrel with the CBC but I don't want to be controlled by my competitor. Newspapers don't have to reserve space for the government; their advertising space isn't being controlled. Broadcasting is a form of publication and should not be so controlled."

On the political front, private broadcasters had found a staunch ally in John George Diefenbaker, leader of the Conservative Party. Although the CBC had been established by a Conservative government, the Tories had long been at odds with the public broadcaster. Much of the mistrust dated back to the Second World War, when the CBC had refused several requests from Conservative leader Arthur Meighen for air-time to offer opposition views on Prime Minister Mackenzie King's wartime policies. To the Conservatives, at least, it appeared the CBC was nothing more than a public relations arm of the Liberal government. In a celebrated speech in Winnipeg in 1942, Meighen slammed both the prime minister and the CBC; "The radio of Canada has been for years, and is today, and Mr. King intends it will continue to be, the effective monopoly, tool and instrument of a partisan government headed by himself."

Diefenbaker had developed the same visceral dislike of the CBC, and took up the cause of private broadcasters with a vengeance. Voice raised and jowls shaking, the Leader of the Opposition hammered away at his nemesis. "Danger to the freedom of speech exists on the radio today," he proclaimed, "with the Canadian Broadcasting Corporation acting as competitor to private radio stations, while also serving as investigator, judge and jury."

The election of 1957 stunned political pundits and the long governing Liberals, as Diefenbaker and his Conservatives were elected with a minority government. A year later, the Tories finished the job, scoring a massive victory taking 208 seats in the House of Commons. One of the early pieces of legislation by the new government was a re-written Broadcasting Act, taking regulatory power away from the CBC and placing it in the hands of a new organization known as the Board of Broadcast Governors. Private broadcasters still faced many rules and restrictions, but they had won a major victory. Years later, the Board of Broadcast Governors would evolve into yet another regulatory agency called the Canadian Radio and Television Commission or CRTC.

Transition

On Friday, November 22, 1963, 25-year-old Ivan LeMesurier (who would become better known as Lee Major) headed to CBW Winnipeg for his first day on the job as a new staff announcer. He had arrived from Churchill just that morning. As he entered his new workplace, it was soon evident this was no ordinary day. US President John Kennedy had been shot in Dallas. "I got down to 541 Portage," recalls LeMesurier, "and (producer) Ross Dobson was supposed to put me through a training session for a week. He gave me a newscast and said you're in booth 20 (broadcasting) to Edmonton. It was a strange opening for me."

Throughout the afternoon, people were glued to their radios for the latest information on one of the darkest days in American history. When the workday was over, they rushed home...to watch the developments on television.

The assassination of John Kennedy was the first major television news event. Radio was taking a back seat. Throughout the decade, television had been gaining momentum. Many of the popular radio sitcoms and dramas had moved to the television screen. In Canada, Saturday night hockey and even professional wrestling had gained a large following. Sales of television sets skyrocketed. The ground had shifted. Radio would have to change its ways.

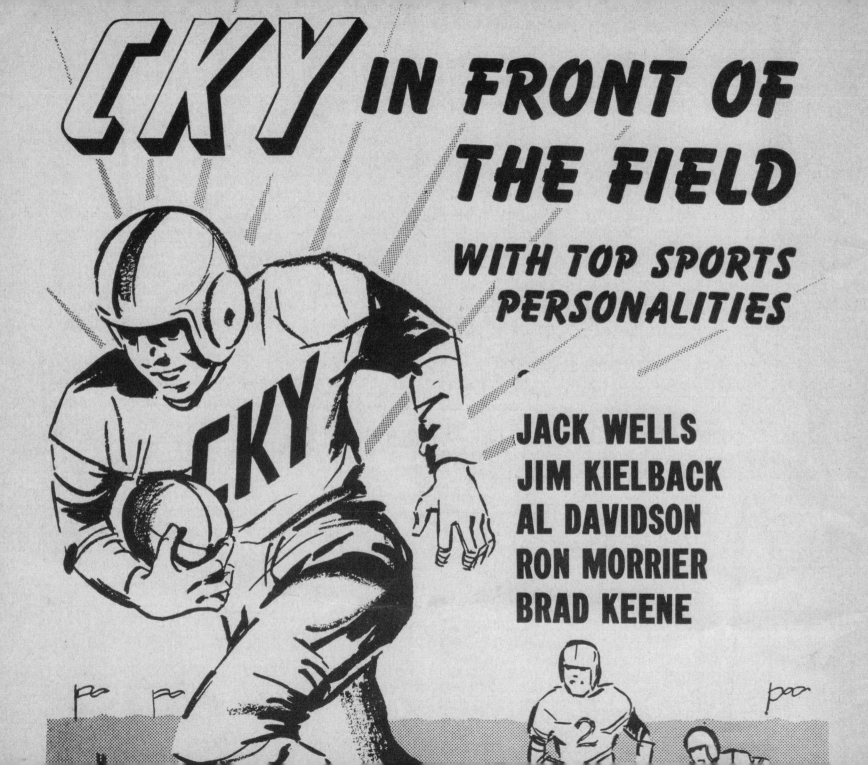

CHAPTER TEN

The Sporting Life

For a generation of fans, the 1950s and '60s represent the Golden Age of sport in Manitoba. The Winnipeg Blue Bombers were in their glory years. In a six-year span, beginning in 1957, the Bombers appeared in five Grey Cups, winning four championships. In 1955, professional hockey returned to Winnipeg, with the minor league Winnipeg Warriors playing in a brand new Winnipeg Arena. The second dominant winter sport was curling. The community curling rink was the centre of social activity in most rural towns, and Manitoba curlers were bringing home national championships. In summer, the sport of choice was baseball, with the Winnipeg Goldeyes affiliated with the major league St. Louis Cardinals.

For radio broadcasters, sports was an easy sell, with broadcast rights relatively inexpensive, if they existed at all. At one point in the 1950s, both CKY and CKRC were providing play-by-play of Blue Bomber football. By the 1960s, CJOB had grabbed the broadcast rights, ultimately becoming the voice of local sports.

Saskatchewan native Johnny Esaw was sports director at CKRC throughout much of the 1950s. Esaw had put in a great deal of hard work and long hours to get to a major market radio station, moving from North Battleford to Regina and then to Winnipeg. Along the way, he had also developed definite opinions about how certain tasks were to be completed. An underling at CKRC was a rookie broadcaster named Ron Oakes. From the perspective of young Oakes, Esaw was a taskmaster. The two clashed continuously. "There's no doubt about it, he made my life miserable," recalled Oakes in an interview years later. It may explain his decision to leave the country. Oakes left Winnipeg to become play-by-play broadcaster for the San Diego Gulls of the Western Hockey League. Among the players he befriended was Willie O'Ree, who would become the first black player in the National Hockey League. When Oakes

Opposite: CKY Sports Promotion.
GARRY MOIR COLLECTION

JOHNNY ON THE SPORT

Whatever the sport—Johnny covers it "like a blanket" with 3 feature sportscasts daily and during the football season listen to:

ESAW & HIS FRIENDS, nightly 6:45 p.m. Featuring on Fridays The Bud Grant Show.

FOOTBALL TIME, Thursday's 9:30 p.m. when W. I. F. U. Sportscasters report.

TOM CASEY'S Football Forum, Friday's 10:30 p.m.

FOOTBALL MONITOR with Johnny Esaw, Tom Casey, Ron Oakes and guests heard before every football broadcast.

AND AFTER EVERY GAME Johnny will have Al Wiley, Ken Charlton, Maurice Smith and other outstanding Football Personalities with post-game comments.

CKRC

THE SPORTS VOICE OF THE RED RIVER VALLEY

died in 2007, O'Ree paid tribute to the former Winnipegger as a first rate sports announcer.

Well-established in Manitoba, with no intention of leaving, Esaw and his wife were relaxing at their cottage on Lake Winnipeg on a summer day in 1960. A little way down the road there was great excitement at the small grocery and convenience store. As part of its service, the business would take messages for cottagers like Esaw, who had no telephone. A call had come for the CKRC sportscaster... and the caller was none other than hockey legend Foster Hewitt. Hewitt wanted Esaw for a position at CFTO television which was soon to go on the air in Toronto. Hewitt was a shareholder in what would become the flagship station for the CTV television network. Esaw would leave CKRC and become a major force in Canadian broadcasting, rising to become a senior executive at CTV. He was instrumental in developing coverage of numerous national and Olympic sporting events, and is widely credited for making figure skating a mainstream sport on television.

R.J. "Bob" Picken interviews Gordie Howe at CJOB. RORY MACLENNAN FAMILY

It was not until the mid-1960s that CJOB hired its first full time sportscaster. His name was R.J. "Bob" Picken, a former writer with the defunct *Winnipeg Citizen* newspaper, who also happened to be one of the province's elite curlers. Early in his career, Picken was in the unique position of reporting on events he was also participating in. He recalls a provincial curling championship at the Winnipeg Arena from which he was filing live reports to the radio station. "I had to do a report at 12:45, and at 12:40 I was still on the ice finishing my game. I virtually had to jump over the boards to get to the radio equipment and was a little bit late in getting on the air, but I got my report done." The "25-after-the-hour sportscast" was launched by Picken and program director Cliff Gardner...a programming concept that lasted 47 years on CJOB. Working for CJOB, and later CBW, Bob Picken became a sports institution in Manitoba in a career that spanned more than four decades. He was skilled at play-by-play coverage of curling and football. Picken called 14 consecutive Grey

Cup games and covered 35 Briers. He also became an influential builder of the world curling championships.

Picken's departure to the CBC in 1969 opened the door for Ken "Friar" Nicolson to join CJOB. The Thunder Bay broadcaster would be the first voice of the Winnipeg Jets of the World Hockey Association, and preside over one of the biggest stories in hockey history when superstar Bobby Hull jumped from the NHL to join the new Winnipeg franchise of the WHA.

CBC Manitoba committed considerable resources to sports coverage throughout the 1950s, '60s and '70s. For a number of years the public broadcaster would set aside regular programming to broadcast the World Series. The CBC also placed particular emphasis on college and amateur sports. In the 1950s, Bob Moir hosted "Prairie Sports Final," a half hour weekly program that ran in Manitoba, Saskatchewan and Alberta. Other sports personalities included Walter Unger, Doug McIlraith, Murray Parker, Phil Reimer and Ernie Nairn. Each of these broadcasters worked in both radio and television and was able to carve his own successful niche at the CBC.

Munich

In 1961, the CBC hired a 25-year-old sportscaster from the small community of Herbert, Saskatchewan, located just east of Swift Current. Don Wittman would become nationally and internationally known for his play-by-play skills in hockey, football and curling, and for his specialty of describing track and field events at competitions around the world. He mastered the craft of calling the 100-metre race. In an event that lasted less than 10 seconds, no one could encapsulate and generate more excitement than Don Wittman.

On September 5, 1972, while most Winnipeggers were still asleep, Wittman was having breakfast with television producer Bob Moir and several others. They were in Munich, Germany as part of the CBC contingent covering the Olympic Games. Word came there had been some type of incident where the Israeli athletes were staying. On foot, Wittman and Moir headed for the Olympic Village. Dodging security guards, they climbed under a fence and headed to the residence where Canadian medical staff was staying. The building directly opposite housed the Israeli team. Eight members of a Palestinian independence group known as Black September had taken 11 Israeli athletes hostage. Talks between the police and the hostage-takers dragged on throughout the day. No journalist in the world was closer to this developing story than Wittman. He phoned reports back to Toronto which were broadcast across the country and the world. At one point, the Winnipeg sportscaster followed a security official onto a balcony where a grey-hooded hostage-taker, only a few yards away, spoke to them. Late in the day, Wittman and others in the Canadian building sought cover as word came a rescue was about to unfold. It was a false alarm, as police and security forces backed down.

Eventually, German security forces agreed that an army bus should be brought in to take the Palestinians and their prisoners to the Munich airport. Wittman watched from no more than 15 yards away as the Israeli athletes, some of them crying, were herded onto the bus. "You just knew something awful was about to happen," recalled Wittman, in a CBC interview years later. It did. A rescue attempt at the airport was a disaster, with all 11 athletes and eight hostage-takers killed.

International sporting events would never be the same. The memories of that dark day would remain with Wittman for the rest of his life.

Cactus

In sharp contrast to Wittman's polished professionalism was the best known sports personality the city ever produced. John Hampton "Cactus Jack" Wells was a true legend...a household name, not only in Manitoba, but across the country. Wells

took radio to places it had never gone before...not always with the best results, but always with a large audience. If even half the stories about Jack Wells are true, he was still one of the most remarkable characters ever to sit in front of a microphone.

Born in 1911, Wells came of age during the Great Depression. His father's contracting business in Moose Jaw failed. Young Jack had dropped out of school in Grade 8 to help his parents. He was regularly seen cycling around Moose Jaw, delivering CPR telegraphs. At night, he apprenticed to become a plumber. In 1936, Canadian Pacific offered Wells a job as a clerk in Saskatoon. Although he didn't know it at the time, the door was opening to a new career.

In Saskatoon, Wells took a room in the local YMCA and began his new job. One evening, he and "a bunch of good guys" were listening to a hockey game. In a burst of youthful hubris, Wells boasted that he could do as good a job as the play-by-play broadcaster on station CFQC. His pals challenged him to prove it. The station was in fact looking for a new sports voice. Wells

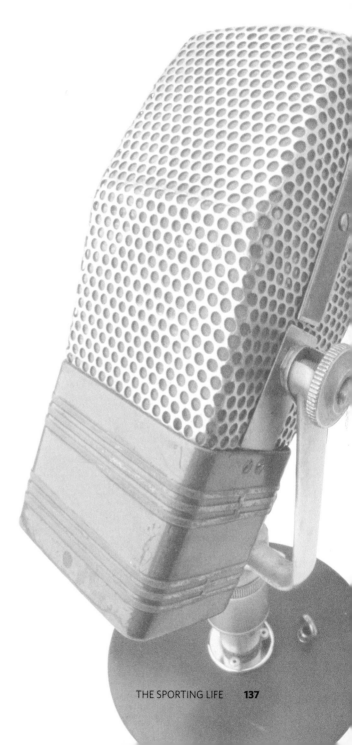

auditioned, and much to his own surprise, got the job. Although he noted later, "broadcasting had never been my ambition," his remarkable career was underway.

Only a short time after being hired, Wells walked into the office of A.A. "Pappy" Murphy, president and owner of CFQC radio. In his hand was a telegram from a radio station in Halifax, offering him a sportscasting job. Murphy, not wanting to look for yet another new announcer, offered to meet the salary being offered by the Maritime station. The CFQC executive never seemed to question how a station as far away as Halifax had heard so quickly about a raw rookie in Saskatoon.

In reality there never was a job offer. Working his former CPR connections, Wells had concocted the entire story, complete with phony telegram. He had also succeeded in getting his first raise in pay. The "pay prank" would become part of Jack Wells lore. His first career move would not be east but west when in 1939 he began a short stint at CJAT radio in Trail, British Columbia.

The outbreak of World War II saw many of Wells' friends and colleagues signing up to join the forces. Wells was apparently ready to go as well but was twice rejected in efforts to enlist because of a heart murmur. Instead, in 1941 he moved to Winnipeg to join CJRC. It would be in Manitoba that his career would take off.

With the war raging and many broadcasters overseas, Wells was called on to perform a multitude of tasks which ranged from country music programming to fundraising events for the troops. What Wells enjoyed the most, however, was chatting up the station's switchboard operator...a young woman named Marguerite Laurson. Wells took to calling her Flicka...exactly why is not clear, although there was a movie called *My Friend Flicka* which made the rounds in 1943. Flicka was a horse, but young Ms. Laurson obviously took it as a term of affection. Marguerite and Jack were married and had three children. Sons John and Richard would eventually have successful broadcasting careers as well.

It was at CJRC that Wells got his first opportunity to do play-by-play football... a game he admittedly knew little about. Although not particularly athletic, he enjoyed sports. As a boy his father had taken him to baseball and hockey games in Saskatchewan. Now he was covering football, hockey, baseball and curling. Cultivating a close relationship with the man who ran both the Winnipeg Amphitheatre and Osborne Stadium, Wells worked a deal which gave him exclusive rights to broadcast from the city's two largest sports venues. This allowed him to leave CJRC and freelance his services to all radio stations in the city. When CBC television arrived, he became Winnipeg's first TV sportscaster. In 1954, CKY radio gave him a contract for exclusive broadcasting rights, which was the start of a long association with the radio station. It was at CKY that he starting calling himself "Cactus Jack" while filling in on a country and western show. He didn't expect it to last, but the moniker stuck. For a period in the 1950s he was doing play-by-play football in both

Cactus Jack Wells carried by his peers at Schmoky fundraising event. WINNIPEG PRESS CLUB COLLECTION

Winnipeg and Regina. On occasion, he would do two games in one day, broadcasting an afternoon match in Regina before flying home to Winnipeg for a night game. He was a regular on Grey Cup broadcasts, a fixture at the McDonald Brier curling championship, and reportedly even turned down an offer to become the play-by-play voice of the Montreal Canadiens.

Whether it was baseball, golf or horse racing, Cactus would be part of it. By 1959, *Maclean's* magazine would report that "because of the scope and variety of Wells' activities it's entirely possible more Canadians have heard him in the last 20 years than any other man this side of Foster Hewitt."

Wells' personality was the key to his success. His devil-may-care attitude toward sportscasting and life in general endeared him to both listeners and co-workers. Wells was a night owl and party guy who survived on his ability to take catnaps anytime, anywhere. Sports-writing colleague, Trent Frayne, once wrote that Wells "is never so happy as when he joins a roomful of raconteurs over a friendly glass, swapping endless

lies about this game or that." The same article went on to describe Jack Wells as "an irreverent rule buster who exudes raffish charm as he mangles the English language and sometimes misinforms his listeners."

Indeed, Wells provided plenty of evidence to back up that assessment. As a CBC Winnipeg announcer in the 1950s, Lloyd Robertson remembers Wells describing a football game where the players were hurling "epitaphs" at each other. When reading the weather forecast on his morning show, he would always provide the "relative humility." Polysyllabic names were an anathema. An often-cited example is Tony Pajaczkowski, a star for the Calgary Stampeders in the 1950s. Tony made many tackles for his team, but rarely got credit on the airwaves. His was a name Wells was not prepared to take a crack at. "My approach to sport is that you've got to have fun," Wells offered in the *Maclean's* interview. "Hell's bells, it's only a game. I figure listeners want to get some entertainment."

Entertain he did, both on and off the air. Pranks and partying became the stuff

of legend. At the Macdonald Brier curling championship, Wells would lead a group of writers and broadcasters in an annual R-rated singsong. He always played a prominent role in developing the lyrics for the group, which was dubbed the Leslie Wells Singers...a takeoff on the popular Leslie Bell Singers of the era. Bob Picken remembers Wells smuggling a live duck into a hotel in Saskatoon and depositing it in the bathtub of a sportswriting colleague. One New Year's Eve, he showed up to do his CBC television sportscast nearly naked... clothed only in a makeshift diaper and a banner across his chest proclaiming himself to be the New Year's baby.

In the early morning hours of November 14, 1954, Wells was sitting in a hotel restaurant near the Edmonton airport. He and the Blue Bombers were waiting to return home after a loss to the Eskimos that knocked Winnipeg out of the playoffs. Hung over after a night of drowning their sorrows, no one on the Bomber squad was in a good mood. Particularly snarly was quarterback Jack Jacobs. "Indian

Jack," as he was known, was nearing the end of his career and there was widespread media speculation that he might have played his final game. There are many versions as to what happened next. Suffice it to say, the "what the hell...it's only a game" attitude of Jack Well didn't sit well that morning. Fists flew, with Jacobs landing at least one blow and probably more to the face of the Winnipeg broadcaster. Bruised and bloodied, Wells made it back to Winnipeg. By all accounts, he and Jacobs had made up before the Bomber airplane arrived back in Winnipeg. At first the local media did not report the story, but when an account of the fight showed up in an Edmonton newspaper it became front page news in Winnipeg as well. For his part, Wells gamely showed up to read the sports on radio. That didn't present a problem, but television was a whole different matter. No amount of makeup could cover his thick lip and facial bruises. CBC Winnipeg received numerous calls asking what on earth had happened to their favourite sportscaster.

"SHE SHOOTS...SHE SCORES!"

By late 1972, plans were in the works for a new radio station in southwestern Manitoba. Less than a year later, CJRB Boissevain was on the air, owned and operated by Radio Southern Manitoba (which would become Golden West Broadcasting). In short order, the station had carved itself a place in sports history.

On November 22, 1975, CJRB aired the first play-by-play broadcast of a women's hockey game. The match was played in Souris, with a championship team from Goodlands taking on a regional all-star team. At the microphone was 22-year-old Dwight MacAulay, who later in life would become the Chief of Protocol for the Province of Manitoba. "I don't really think it dawned on me until after the fact that it was groundbreaking," says McAulay. "There was no press box; you were just out there in the stands and the cold and did your best." Fittingly, the hockey broadcast aired during International Women's Year, as declared by the United Nations.

The fact the fight made newspaper headlines across the country was testimony to Wells' star power. There was, however, considerably more substance to Jack Wells than he was often given credit for. He was by no means oblivious to his limitations. "He was very much aware he had cut off his schooling early," noted brother Eric Wells, in an interview in the late 1950s. "I suppose he felt he had to overcome that." In his own way, Cactus understood exactly what was expected of him. In modern vernacular, it would be described as the "Wells brand." He treated sportscasting as it was meant to be...fun, entertaining and not be taken too seriously. Sports was simply a few hours of escapism in an era of superpower sabre rattling. On his morning broadcasts, a hungover Cactus often sounded like many people felt. He was everyman, and listeners could easily identify. In his prime, few broadcasters had a sharper wit than Cactus Jack.

Wells' networking skills were unprecedented as he developed important relationships with people who could advance his career. For many years, Imperial Tobacco insisted he be part of the Grey Cup broadcasts. The reason was simple, as once stated by Bob Fitzpatrick, a senior executive of the company: "he sells our product." Yet, former colleagues unanimously agree he was anything but a social climber. "He treated everyone the same, right down to the cleaning lady," recalls Embree McDermid, a longtime co-worker at both CJRC and CKY. Rookie broadcaster Jim McSweeney remembers his first days on the job at CKRC. "Jack was the only one who really bothered to speak to me."

Rarely calling anyone by their first name, Wells was a master at nicknames. CKY co-host Don Kirton was "Suet Sam," Blue Bomber star Jerry James was tagged "Kid Dynamite," while another longtime Bomber play-by-play man, Bob Irving of CJOB, was dubbed "Knuckles" because of an aversion to flying. Signature Wellsian phrases such as "it turned out nice again" and "true unbiased report" became part of everyday conversation. Even in later years, Wells' presence was still being felt and heard around the Winnipeg Stadium. His final job on CJOB football broadcasts was to select a player of the game. If fans leaving the stadium liked the choice, they were expected to honk their horns. The so-called "Happy Honker Award" was vintage Jack Wells.

"It was never my ambition to become a broadcaster," reflected Wells in a 1980s CBC interview, "and I guess I never was... but I must say I enjoyed it immensely."

Booze

The Jack Wells story also serves to illustrate a darker side of the radio industry. The issue was alcohol. Certainly the problem was not unique to sportscasters, nor was every broadcaster over-consuming. Drinking, however, was widespread throughout the business, often to the detriment of listeners, advertisers and the broadcasters themselves. "Everywhere you went there was booze," recalled Gus Nanton, an admitted alcoholic, and later a spokesperson for

Alcoholics Anonymous before his death in 1997. "Most of the time it was free," remembers Jim McSweeny of his days at CKRC. Don Kirton paid the price of losing his job because of alcohol. CFRY owner Digby Hughes fought alcoholic demons. Michael Hopkins, who came to Winnipeg via CHUM Toronto, also ran a radio school out of his home. A former student recalls Hopkins meeting his class in his bathrobe, barely able to function because of a severe hangover. Jack Wells and his cronies had their own table at the Criterion Hotel, just behind the CKY building at 432 Main Street. The regular gathering was most often referred to as the "Criterion Athletic Club." Kirton's description of a day in the life of Jack Wells offers considerable insight into how alcohol permeated so many aspects of a broadcaster's job.

"We'd finish the morning show and then go over and have a couple of beers, then he'd go over and do a sports package at CBC, then he'd be off to a golf tournament where he'd be playing and be master of ceremonies or something else and he'd have a few more (drinks). Then back to the CBC and at night he'd often take off after that and maybe MC a fundraiser somewhere."

The outcome of such partying was not always pleasant A young CKY producer was severely assaulted by a station salesman after a bout of heavy drinking. Staff would fail to show up for work. There were also occasions when announcers should never have been on the air.

There's no simple explanation for the phenomenon. Alcohol consumption was very much part of the popular culture throughout the era. For whatever reason, radio attracted some "strange characters," some of whom had been plagued by alcohol abuse long before they entered the industry. Radio could be a transient business with little job security. On-air staff would frequently move from station to station, as this was the most effective way to obtain a raise in pay. It was not unusual to find broadcasters from the 1950s and '60s who had, at one time or another, worked for most radio stations in the city. Getting fired was an accepted part of the business...in some cases almost a badge of honour. Announcers and disc-jockeys lived and died by ratings. Purges were common, as a newly-arrived program director would attempt to give the station a new sound and, hopefully, more listeners. If it didn't work, he was gone too.

Drinking was the unofficial sport of the era. The celebrity status and party atmosphere ultimately took its toll. Jobs were lost, families suffered and more than a few broadcasters died young.

CHAPTER ELEVEN

The Men with the Music

On a Saturday night in late April, 1960, a high school dance was held in Snowflake, Manitoba... a tiny farm village, nearly a three-hour drive southwest of Winnipeg. A big city band, Mickey Brown and the Velvetones, was providing the music, but the real attraction was the appearance of Peter Jackson, a CKY announcer, better known as "P.J. the Dee Jay." Carloads of teenagers from around the region began arriving early in the evening and kept coming. Although no more than 70 people lived in Snowflake at the time, the town's population tripled that night.

"An overcapacity crowd in the community hall" is how the local newspaper described it. Jackson's arrival produced screams and scrambling as he flicked "45 records" into the crowd like Frisbees. He was what the teenagers had come to see. Even in a remote farm community, the disc jockey could draw a crowd.

Peter Jackson was but one of Winnipeg's early celebrity disc jockeys. The late 1950s and early '60s saw radio shifting focus as it scrambled to find its place in a world that now included television. For radio broadcasters, rock 'n' roll could not have arrived at a more opportune time. The genre provided something unique and trendy. The golden-voiced Jackson represented a new wave of broadcasters whose task it was to appeal to a young audience, hopefully with money to spend. Radio was moving away from being all things to all people. During the 1960s, three of Winnipeg's five English language radio stations would try their hand at rock 'n' roll.

The changing taste in music was by no means a local phenomenon. In the United States, an announcer named Allan Freed was attracting huge audiences with a music mix of rhythm and blues and country...aka rock 'n' roll. Later, Freed would find himself in the centre of radio's payola scandal where disc jockeys were receiving money from the music industry or individual

Opposite: The American Invasion...DJs Chuck Dan, Jimmy Darrin, Gary Todd and Dean Scott with Everly Brothers. CKY REUNION ARCHIVES

artists to play their songs. In Mexico, just a few miles from the US border, a young DJ who would come to be known as Wolfman Jack was howling his way to North American fame. At 1050 CHUM in Toronto, the airwaves were never the same after owner Alan Waters moved to follow an American format providing "hit parade" music day and night. CHUM's success did not go unnoticed in the rest of the country.

Manitobans, like people everywhere, were deeply divided on the subject of rock

'n' roll. So too were local broadcasters. For some, it truly was the "devil's music." CFAM music director Ben Horch pulled no punches, describing "hit parade in every degree and in every form from the mildest to the most extreme varieties through and through anti-Christian, anti-culture."

The changing taste in music was also unsettling for more than a few on-air personalities. When CKY began shifting to "hit parade" music, country music promoter Porky Charbonneau packed up

and temporarily left the radio business. In Regina, jazz aficionado Gren Marsh was not impressed with CKCK's switch to rock 'n' roll. He moved to CBW Winnipeg as a staff announcer beginning a career that spanned more than 30 years.

Another broadcaster who had no time for this new sound was CJOB's John Oliver Blick. Not that his station didn't try it out. Program director George Davies returned from a conference in the United States armed with a new format which included a dose of rock 'n' roll. "Jack Blick just about went crazy," recalled Phil Isley, an announcer at the station. On September 26, 1959, Blick ran a full page ad in both Winnipeg newspapers, declaring CJOB had banned rock 'n' roll. The station pledged to avoid "raucous rock 'n' roll like the plague" with Jack Blick offering the following explanation for the station's decision:

"People today are hungry for music, but there are many radios in Manitoba standing silent most of the time because their owners want

sounds they can enjoy...not beeps, thumps, crashes and twangs.

Our crusade for sing and whistle music stems from our strong personal conviction that radio listeners of all ages want good music. They will get it on CJOB, and we expect many silent radios will be switched on to welcome the change."

Over the years, many listeners did switch their radios to CJOB, but not even Jack Blick could deny the rapidly growing appeal of rock 'n' roll music. In 1958, Ray St. Germain used CKY studios to record a song entitled "She's a Square." Lenny Breau was part of the group that provided backup on guitar while the station's engineer Andy Melownchuk handled technical matters. CKY would later claim "She's a Square" was the first rock 'n' roll song ever played in Winnipeg. It reached #7 on the CKY hit parade.

By the early 1960s, Winnipeg laid claim to literally hundreds of bands trying out the new genre. Every weekend, teenagers would flock to community clubs and high

Personality driven radio: CKRC.
CAVIN BORODY AND GARRY MOIR COLLECTION

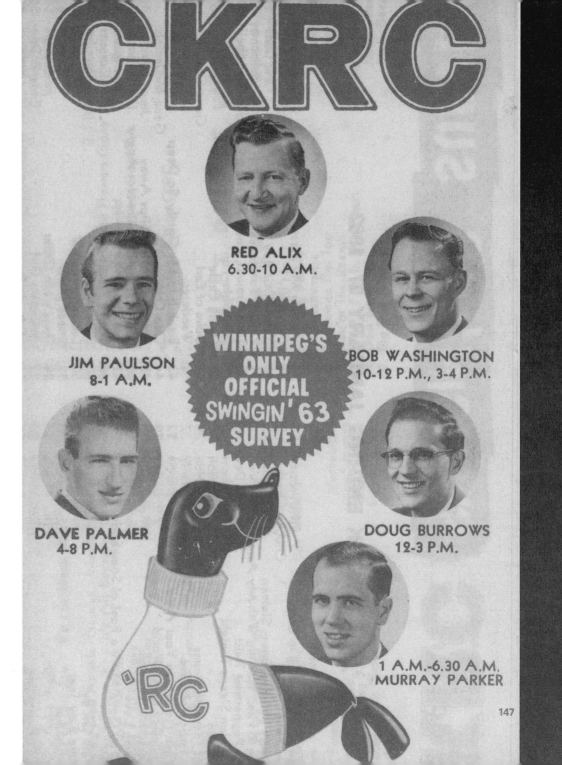

CKRC

RED ALIX
6.30-10 A.M.

JIM PAULSON
8-1 A.M.

BOB WASHINGTON
10-12 P.M., 3-4 P.M.

WINNIPEG'S ONLY OFFICIAL SWINGIN' 63 SURVEY

DAVE PALMER
4-8 P.M.

DOUG BURROWS
12-3 P.M.

'RC

1 A.M.-6.30 A.M.
MURRAY PARKER

MANITOBA'S

CKY

5000 WATTS
FIRST ON THE
DIAL AT 580

432 MAIN STREET
WINNIPEG, CANADA

WINNEPEG MANITOBA...

APR. 29TH. 1959.

HI DON.

AS FAR AS I KNOW THE SONG AND SINGER YOU ARE
WONDERING ABOUT IS HIGH NOON SUNG BY FRANKIE LAINE.
I DONT KNOW OF ANY OTHER SONG IN THE PICTURE AND
FRANKIE LAINE HAD A GOLD RECORD OF HIGH NOON ON
THE HIT PARADE A FEW YEARS BACK. I HOPE THIS IS
THE INFO YOU WERE LOOKING FOR. P.S. EXCUSE LOUSY
TYPING I'M IN A HE... OF A HURRY....

SO LONG......

school sock hops to see groups with strange sounding names like The Jury, The Shags and The Deverons. The girls would stand on one side of the room while the boys languished on the other, each lad in his own way trying to work up his courage to ask someone to dance. "I can tell you I got turned down many times," recalls Gord Hudson, a teenager in the 1960s. Hudson also remembers a high school dance at Silver Heights Collegiate, featuring The Deverons, when a band member jumped on the piano and "cut loose" with his guitar. "We all stopped dancing just to watch him perform," Hudson recalls. The young performer was Burton Cummings, who would go on to be known around the world as lead singer of The Guess Who.

But the teenagers came to see more than just the local band. Part of any dance action was a disc jockey from the local rock 'n' roll radio station. Radio was driving rock, and stations were willing to pay good money for top voices as a means of attracting a larger audience. P.J. the Dee Jay was one of many personality disc jockeys. Dennis "Deno"

Corrie, Ron "Keg" Legge, Bob Bradburn, Daryl B, "Doc" Steen, Marc Parr, Mal Faris, Boyd Kozak and numerous others were household names for most teenagers. In some cases, the DJs were as popular as the bands. "If Deno Corrie or Daryl B or Marc Parr...if they were going to be there, we wanted to be there too," recalls Hudson from his teenage years.

As long as the disc jockeys stuck within the parameters of their format, they could pretty much play whatever they wished, and playing local music helped build an audience. The most successful bands of the era were those that formed some type of affiliation with a local disc jockey. Connecting with the right DJ could be a significant career move. Regardless of how good they might be, the artists needed airplay and promotion. That's where the disc jockey came in. Joey Gregorash, a future CKY disc jockey, headed a group called The Mongrels. "The more you got them (the DJs) on your bandwagon, the better it was for you, and obviously it was influential because they would be talking about you," recalls Gregorash.

One group went so far as to anoint themselves the Club 63 Galaxies...a play on CKRC's 630 spot on the AM dial.

The bands and the disc jockeys were intertwined, each needing the other. For example, Dennis Corrie was closely associated with Al and the Silvertones, which became Chad Allan and the Expressions, which became Chad Allan and the Reflections, which evolved into The Guess Who. Corrie would promote the bands and make public appearances while Guess Who "world premiere" recordings were heard on his show.

21-year-old Daryl Burlingham arrived in Winnipeg via CFQC in Saskatoon. As a youngster, he had battled polio. Lingering effects of the disease would contribute to his death at an early age. In 1964, however, Daryl B was riding the wave of rock 'n roll, working at CKRC before moving over to CKY.

The young man from Saskatoon had much going for him. Blessed with a naturally rich, resonant, high energy sound, Burlingham was more than ready for big market radio. "He looked exactly like he

Daryl Burlingham.
CKY REUNION ARCHIVES

sounded," said longtime colleague and friend Boyd Kozak. "Tall, dark and handsome and confidence like you wouldn't believe." Like many of his contemporaries, he was deeply into the music. Late one night at CKY studios at 432 Main Street, Daryl B helped produce the Deverons' first recording.

Burlingham also had close ties with a group known as "The Jury." "Daryl was very serious on the air and was actually more into the music he was playing than he was into being a big personality," says George Johns, a member of the group. "I don't actually ever remember him laughing; he always just smiled." Johns also worked at CKY, serving as board operator for the nightly "Daryl B Show" from Champs Kentucky Fried Chicken locations at Inkster and McPhillips and on Henderson Highway. The program, with its latest pop tunes, local bands, high school teen tipsters and B's omnipresent bicycle horn attracted youth from all over Winnipeg. "There was just an aura about him," recalled former Winnipeg broadcaster Warren Cosford.

"It was not an act, he didn't say too many words...he just had an aura."

Winnipeg served as a launching pad for Cosford, Johns and Burlingham. Johns went on to a successful career as a program director in both Canada and United States. Cosford became an award-winning producer in Toronto. Burlingham emerged as one of the elite disc jockeys in the continent, working at CHUM Toronto, CFUN Vancouver and CKLW Windsor...a border station programming not only to Canada but also to Detroit and a huge American audience. He was ultimately courted by KHJ radio in Los Angeles, although he never made the move to Hollywood. While Daryl B had cranked up his persona from the early days in Winnipeg, his prairie reserve would always be part of his personality. "I don't know many people who were close to Daryl," says Cosford, who would work with Burlingham at CHUM. "It wasn't that he was not friendly, but he wasn't someone who opened up about himself very much." The Daryl B "mystique" could prove powerfully appealing. "Daryl B always had at least one

CKRC disc jockeys on parade. Don Slade centre, "Doc" Steen right and Jim Paulson on left. SHARON MCRAE

gorgeous woman in his life, usually two or three. He had a tumultuous private life." "He was running pretty fast," says Kozak. "He was into a lot of things, living the so-called life...which in the end was sad."

CKRC also had its stable of personality disc jockeys...among them, Jim Paulson, who interviewed local bands from the Paddlewheel Restaurant on the sixth floor of the Hudson's Bay store. On Saturday afternoons, it was simply the place to be. On week nights it was Boyd Kozak,

"Ma Kozak's Favorite Middle Son," playing the hits from the Red Top Restaurant on St. Mary's Road. Kozak, born of immigrant parents from Ukraine, grew up in Wadena, Saskatchewan listening to late night radio from distant American stations like WLS Chicago. On being hired for his first job in Weyburn, young Boris, as he was then known, was informed by the station manager he would have to change his name. "Boris Kozak is not conducive to good English radio" is how Kozak recalls the conversation. "My Dad went right through the ceiling." A compromise was reached. Boris became Boyd. Kozak launched a successful career and would lay claim to the title of the great survivor of Winnipeg radio. Fifty years after being hired by CKRC, he was still on the air.

Morning host Bob Bradburn developed close ties to a group called the Squires and their lead singer Neil Young. The Squires' first record was produced at CKRC. The songs were Young originals, titled "The Sultan" and "Aurora." According to one Young biography, it is Bradburn who can

CHUMS

From the late 1960s through the '70s, CHUM radio in Toronto was Canada's rock 'n' roll powerhouse. The station had massive influence over record sales and the success or failure of individual groups or artists. CHUM, along with CKLW Windsor and a handful of US stations, were setting the standard for rock radio. "There were stations in the (United) States and Canada trying to mirror what CHUM was doing," says former Winnipeg producer Bob McMillan, who worked at CHUM. "They had a huge influence."

Who were the programmers, producers and creative writers behind CHUM's success? To no small degree, they were former Manitobans who cut their teeth in Winnipeg radio. The staff at CHUM read like a Manitoba broadcasters' reunion. Leading the way was J. Robert Wood, who had worked at CKY in its glory years. Bob Wood, raised in Teulon, was cited by *Billboard Magazine* as one of the top programmers in North America. Production Manager Warren Cosford arrived at CHUM via CJOB. Creative Director Bill McDonald was also a CJOB alumnus. Bob McMillan got his first radio job at CKY. Wood, Cosford, McMillan and McDonald were instrumental in the production of CHUM's award-winning rock documentaries on "The Story of the Beatles," "The Elvis Story" and "The Evolution of Rock." The documentaries were heard around the world, and were still playing on radio stations 40 years later.

Other Manitobans on the memorable CHUM roster included Rick Halson (CKY), Mike Kornfeld (CJOB), John Tucker (CKY), Ken Porteous (CFAR), Chuck McCoy (CKY) and Daryl Burlingham (CKRC-CKY).

Fabulous Fifty Survey

WEEK OF MAY 16th, 1964

'KY GOOD GUYS

Jack Wells

George Dawes

Wild Willie Grogan

Donn Kirton

Daryl B

Jimmy Darin

Dennis Corrie

Gary Todd

Mark Parr

	THIS WEEK	LAST WEEK
1	MISERY - Beatles	1
2	IT'S OVER - Ray Orbison	4
3	BITS & PIECES Dave Clark Five	3
4	ROMEO & JULIET Reflections	12
5	CROOKED LITTLE MAN Serendipity	2
6	LOVE ME WITH ALL YOUR HEART - Ray Charles Singers	16
7	NEEDLES & PINS - Searchers	6
8	CHAPEL OF LOVE Dixie Cups	19
9	LONG TALL SALLY - Beatles	7
10	MY GIRL SLOOPY Vibrations	13
11	WORLD WITHOUT LOVE Peter & Gordon Also - Bobby Rydell	24
12	RONNIE - Four Seasons	20
13	DIANE - Bachelors	9
14	WHITE ON WHITE Danny Williams	5
15	LITTLE CHILDREN Billy Kramer	18
16	THE FRENCH SONG Lucille Starr	40
17	WHAT'D I SAY - Monarchs	17
18	AIN'T THAT JUST LIKE ME - Searchers	22
19	VERY THOUGHT OF YOU Rick Nelson	21
20	EBB TIDE - Lenny Welch	14
21	TODAY - New Christy Minstrels	28
22	HELLO DOLLY Louis Armstrong	8
23	VIVA LAS VEGAS Elvis Presley	30
24	P.S. I LOVE YOU - Beatles	10
25	SHANGRI-LA Robert Maxwell	15

	THIS WEEK	LAST WEEK
26	THAT'S THE WAY BOYS ARE - Lesley Gore	11
27	KISS ME QUICK Elvis Presley	33
28	CHARADE - Sammy Kaye	29
29	WINKIN' BLINKIN' & NOD Simon Sisters	25
30	I'M THE LONELY ONE Cliff Richard	38
31	3 WINDOW COUPE Rip Cords	39
32	NOT FADE AWAY Rolling Stones	37
33	BABY BEETLE WALK Al Martin Six	47
34	TALL COOL ONE - Wailers	41
35	THIS BOY - Beatles	23
36	SHAKE THAT LITTLE FOOT Round Robin	46
37	WORLD OF LONELY PEOPLE Anita Bryant	43
38	DEAD MAN'S CURVE Jan & Dean	26
39	WRONG FOR EACH OTHER Andy Williams	—
40	GONNA GET ALONG Davis - Dey	48
41	NADINE - Chuck Berry	45
42	PEOPLE - Barbara Streisand	—
43	I DON'T WANT TO BE HURT Nat Cole	34
44	SHOOP SHOOP SONG Betty Everett	27
45	YESTERDAY'S HERO Gene Pitney	49
46	MY BOY LOLLIPOP Millie Small	—
47	MATADOR - Major Lance	32
48	TEARS - Al Martino ROSES	—
49	I'LL TOUCH A STAR Terry Stafford	—
50	MY GUY - Mary Wells	50

Top 20 C & W

1	THE FRENCH SONG Lucille Starr	1
2	BREAKFAST WITH THE BLUES - Hank Snow	6
3	GIRL FROM SPANISH TOWN - Marty Robbins	2
4	LOOK WHO'S TALKING Jim Reeves & Dottie West	4
5	TIMBER I'M FALLING Ferlin Husky	3
6	KEEPING UP WITH THE JONES' - Faron Young & Margie Singleton	7
7	LONG GONE LONESOME BLUES - Hank Williams Jr.	5
8	MEMORY No. 1 Webb Pierce	11
9	SORROW ON THE ROCKS Porter Wagoner	10
10	KEEP THOSE CARDS & LETTERS COMING IN Johnny & Jonie Mosby	14
11	MY HEART SKIPS A BEAT TOGETHER AGAIN Buck Owens	8
12	THIS WHITE CIRCLE Kitty Wells	9
13	UNDERSTAND YOUR MAN Johnny Cash	12
14	THAT'S WHAT MAKES THE WORLD GO ROUND Claude King	13
15	YESTERDAY - Roy Drusky	17
16	SAGINAW, MICHIGAN Lefty Frizzell	16
17	MOLLY - Eddy Arnold	15
18	WHEN THE WORLD'S ON FIRE - Tillman Franks Singers	20
19	HEART - Stu Phillips HERE SHE COMES AGAIN	19
20	MILLERS CAVE Bobby Bare	18

— BEATLETALK —

MISERY, LONG TALL SALLY both on KY Country's biggest Album "LONG TALL SALLY" by the Beatles

Winnipeg's Official Better Music Survey

COMPILED AS A FREE PUBLIC SERVICE BY CKY

be heard whispering "Aurora" throughout the recording.

On an April evening in 1964, the Squires hauled their guitars and drums up the stairs to the second floor of the *Free Press* building where CKRC studios were located. Producer Harry Taylor would be the first to record Neil Young and his upstart band. In fact, many young groups cut their recording teeth under the guidance of Taylor. "In retrospect, it was a primitive undertaking," recalled Taylor years later. "I only had one track, we would lay down the instruments and then dub the voices on later but not on a separate track; we'd have to dub it over to another tape machine. So your noise level was constantly going up and it was quite a thing to try to hold down the tape hiss and get anything out of the instruments." With Taylor's hand at the dials and watching sound levels, Neil Young sat on the piano and played his guitar. What happened next would be a story Taylor would tell for the rest of his life. "Neil came into the control room and asked 'well what do ya think?' I didn't want to put them down or anything

like that, I tried to be as diplomatic as possible. I said I loved the song, you're a great guitar player but I don't think you'll make it as a singer."

The debate over which disc jockey was the most influential is a subjective one. However, the name of one individual surfaces regularly as local musicians look back on the era. Irving "Doc" Steen is credited by many to have forwarded their careers. A native of Winnipeg, Steen had visions of becoming a pharmacist...hence the nickname "Doc." Given his deep voice and mellifluous tones, he decided radio was a better prescription for his life. Hired by CJOB in the late 1950s, he went to work at CKGM Montreal before returning to CKRC as a rock 'n' roll disc jockey. On air, he developed his own unique schtick. Shying away from bells, whistles and sound effects, Steen instead collected a number of short sound bites of characters saying rather strange things. During the course of his show, he would drop in these voices seemingly any time he felt like it and then proceed to carry on a conversation. Doc could be reading

the weather forecast when suddenly a voice would interrupt saying "I ate a sandwich." Steen would tell the voice to bring him one too and proceed with regular programming.

Steen arrived at CKRC just as Winnipeg's community club scene hit full stride. "I guess for a span of about three or four years I was out every Friday and Saturday night emceeing the dances," he remembered in a 1997 CBC interview. "They would pay us for it. I think it was worthwhile for them to pay us for it. It was a tough way to make a few bucks, (there was) a lot of pot floating around, you could smell the stuff a mile away."

In many respects, Steen was almost a father figure to the young band members. In 1964, he turned 40, making him considerably older than many of his colleagues. He was also married, his wife Anne coming from a family with close connections to the Conservative party. (Anne Steen ran as a Conservative Party candidate in the 1972 and 1974 federal elections. Her brother Nathan Nurgitz was President of the Progressive Conservative Party of Canada

and was appointed to the Senate.) At a time of hard partying and "free love," Steen provided a maturity that was not always evident among some other broadcasters.

Musical legend Randy Bachman recalls Steen giving him records that CKRC no longer used or wanted. In one biography, former Guess Who member Jim Kale described Steen as "a bloody saint." "He certainly helped a lot of local bands," said former colleague Bob Washington, when Doc Steen passed away in 2004.

If there was any question about radio's power to mobilize teenagers, it was put to rest on August 18, 1964. By 1:35 that warm afternoon, a Pan American Lockheed Elekra jet began its descent for a routine refuelling stop at Winnipeg International Airport. Contact had been made with the Winnipeg control tower. The aircraft was expected to be on the ground no more than 20 minutes to half an hour before continuing its lengthy journey from London, England to Los Angeles. While such refuelling stops were hardly unique, what was out of the ordinary was who was on board.

The plane was carrying the Beatles. They were heading to California to begin their second tour of North America. The morning had passed quietly without the slightest inkling the Fab Four might be putting in an appearance.

Shortly before 1:30, word was spreading in media circles that the plane would be touching down in Winnipeg. "A quarter of an hour before the plane arrived, news of their arrival was reported on one or two radio stations," according to the *Free Press*. It is almost certain those stations were CKY and CKRC, as both outlets had reporters at the airport when the plane touched down. As the Beatles' jet was preparing for its approach into Winnipeg, Bruce Decker, a teenager who lived on Moray Street, was thinking of heading to the beach with some friends. Hearing radio reports of the Beatles' imminent arrival, they made a beeline for the airport. By the time the Beatles' plane touched down at 2:05, more than a thousand screaming youngsters were jammed into the observation deck, some even making it to the

CKRC'S OFFICIAL TOP FORTY

FEBRUARY 14th — FEBRUARY 21st

TW		LW	TW	
1	BUILD ME UP BUTTERCUP	31	20	THIS GIRL'S IN LOVE WITH YOU
	—The Foundations			—Dionne Warwick
2	TOUCH ME—The Doors	13	21	WORST THAT COULD HAPPEN
3	CRIMSON & CLOVER—Tommy James			—Brooklyn Bridge
4	THIS MAGIC MOMENT	14	22	THESE EYES—Guess Who
	—Jay & The Americans	39	23	TIME OF THE SEASON—The Zombies
5	SWEET CREAM LADIES—The Box Tops	9	24	I STARTED A JOKE—Bee Gees
6	EVERYDAY PEOPLE—Sly & Family Stone	19	25	CINNAMON—Derek
7	RAMBLIN GAMBLIN MAN	34	26	LILY THE PINK—Irish Rovers/Scaffold
	—Bob Seger System	35	27	CLOSE THE BARN DOOR—49th Parallel
8	CRUEL WAR—Sugar & Spice	20	28	IF I CAN DREAM—Elvis Presley
9	PROUD MARY	29	29	BABY, BABY DON'T CRY—The Miracles
	—Creedence Clearwater Revival	37	30	HELLO IT'S ME—Nazz
10	BUT YOU KNOW I LOVE YOU	21	31	SON OF A PREACHER MAN
	—First Edition			—Dusty Springfield
11	GAMES PEOPLE PLAY—Joe South	22	32	BABY LET'S WAIT—Royal Guardsmen
12	YOU SHOWED ME—The Turtles	33	33	HEY BABY—Jose Feliciano
13	CAN I CHANGE MY MIND	38	34	SOULSHAKE—Peggy & Jo Jo
	—Tyrone Davis	36	35	CONDITION RED—Goodees
14	STAND BY YOUR MAN	—	36	TRACES—Classics IV
	—Tammy Wynette	—	37	TO SUSAN ON THE WEST COAST
15	WOMAN HELPING MAN—The Vogues			—Donovan
16	DIZZY—Tommy Roe	—	38	HEAVEN—Rascals
17	INDIAN GIVER—1910 Fruitgum Co.	40	39	MAY I—Bill Deal
18	CROSSROADS—Cream	—	40	WITCHI TAI TO
19	I'M LIVIN IN SHAME—Supremes			—Everything is Everything

DON SLADE

Today on my show we'll discuss the drinking habits of the South American grasshopper.

DOC STEEN

Working during my lunch hour has its advantages. I get the rest of the day off.

BOYD KOZAK

Today's question is worth forty-five pickles. Who was the first Ukrainian to swim Sturgeon Creek?

PICK HIT OF THE WEEK

THE WEIGHT
Aretha Franklin

CANADA TOP FIVE

1. CRUEL WAR—Sugar and Spice
2. THESE EYES—Guess Who
3. CLOSE THE BARN DOOR—49th Parallel
4. SUNSHINE PEOPLE—The Fifth
5. SO COME WITH ME—Witness

TONKIN

I wish Christie would stop leaving his lunch in the control room. I'm getting sick of grape sandwiches.

DARELL PROVOST

Be sure to set your alarm for three a.m. every morning. You'll hear my best newscast.

JIM CHRISTIE

I went ice fishing on Tuesday. I caught lots of ice but threw it all back.

GARY HART

I used to be an animal trainer. One of my better ones was Eric Burden.

CKRC Young at Heart Charts.
CAVIN BORODY AND GARRY MOIR COLLECTION

tarmac. The swooning, screaming and tears reached a fever pitch as Paul McCartney became the first Beatle to step on Canadian soil, followed by John Lennon, George Harrison and Ringo Starr.

Although the mop-top quartet didn't realize it, Winnipeg had already carved itself a place in Beatles history. Less than two years earlier, in late November of 1962, CKY's Dennis "Deno" Corrie had aired a song recorded in Germany on his Sunday morning world music show. The artist was British entertainer Tony Sheridan and backing him up was a group referred to as the Beat Brothers, also known as the Silver Beetles. Band members included John Lennon, Paul McCartney and George Harrison. "That was the first time a Beatles song aired in North America," claims Corrie. (A number of other North American disc jockeys have also claimed to be the first to play a Beatles song. Most dates are later than the CKY program but exactly which station was the first is all but impossible to verify.)

As the Beatles stepped onto the tarmac, a number of reporters moved forward in an impromptu gathering that would be a career highlight. CKY's Frank Roberts and Michael Hopkins were there, as was Teen Dance Party host Bob Burns from CJAY TV. Sharon McRae, a CKRC librarian, was also there and remembers "it was unreal...as all the reporters were pushing and shoving to get an interview." As police sweated to keep the crowd under control, the Beatles themselves babbled away about not much of anything. The *Free Press* reported that Ringo seemed to be the only one to take the questions seriously. Thirty-five minutes after landing, the aircraft was back in the air, but not before young Decker sprinted barefoot across the tarmac and halfway up the stairs to the plane before being scooped up by authorities and hauled away. A police officer later admitted to the *Tribune* that "it was a little embarrassing having to tell the kids to stop kissing the runway after the plane had left."

As the so called "British music invasion" swept across North America, an American invasion of sorts arrived at CKY. The station invested heavily in US disc-jockeys, hoping to boost its audience... among them, program director Jim Hilliard, known on-air as Jimmy Darrin. Under Hilliard, CKY saw some of its slickest formatting, which included snappy jingles, sound effects, continuous hit music, short punchy newscasts and limited DJ patter.

No local radio station personified the rock 'n' roll era more than CKY. Youthful hubris knew no bounds. The station promoted itself as "Canada's Friendly Giant" and Winnipeg as "western Canada's entertainment capital." Engineer Andy Melownchuk maintained a crisp signal which boomed out of the 50,000 watt transmitter across the province and into Saskatchewan, northwestern Ontario, Minnesota, North Dakota and Montana. On a good night, the CKY signal could be picked up in Chicago and other distant American cities.

While his stay in Winnipeg was brief, Hilliard's influence was lasting. CKY built a huge young audience. Among his hires was a youthful jock called J. Robert Wood, who was raised in Teulon. At the apex of his career, Wood was considered one of the top programmers in North America because of his success at CHUM Toronto. Along with Hilliard, other disc jockeys from the US included Gary Todd, Dean Scott and Charles Daniel Hanks whose on-air name was Chuck Dann. For staunch Canadian nationalists, their worst fears about private broadcasting had come true. Nor was everyone at CKY enthused at having US broadcasters telling them what to do. "Yankee hatchet men" is how former CKY newscaster Vic Edwards remembers the era. "This is Manitoba for goodness sakes, not California."

No group of radio broadcasters before or since has reached the celebrity status of the 1960s disc jockeys. "We got fan mail and signed autographs," remembers Dennis Corrie. "It was an amazing time." Female fans would call the radio stations or flock to events the deejays were attending. On occasion they would even show up at the studio. In the vernacular of the DJs, they were "hit line honeys." The hit line was open 24 hours a day and "if you wished to talk to a

SEEKAYWYE, MANITOBA

Radio stations have a long history of unusual and bizarre publicity stunts. Near the top of any list would be an idea concocted by CKY in 1964 to have a local town named after itself. The concept was simple enough. If a town agreed to change its name to SeeKayWye, the radio station would promote the community as a tourist destination. CKY first approached Binscarth, but the proposal was narrowly defeated in a referendum. The ski resort village of La Riviere proved more fertile ground. By a vote of 139 to 81, property owners approved the plan. Not so fast, countered opponents. Among those fighting the proposal was the Manitoba Historical Society. The provincial government didn't think much of the idea either. "I think the whole thing is a lot of nonsense," was the response of Manitoba's Minister of Natural Resources, Sterling Lyon, in one media interview. A main argument against the proposal was that there should be no commercial context in place names. The cause was not helped when someone directly translated the Cree word SeeKayWye to mean "he voids urine."

For a time CKY did promote La Riviere as a place to see. Hundreds flocked to the ski hill one Saturday to meet "KY Good Guys" Jimmy Darrin, Gary Todd and Marc Parr. On that particular weekend, the town was unofficially referred to as SeeKayWye, Manitoba.

In the end, a government committee on geographic names rejected the idea of a name change. CKY changed its format and focus...and La Riviere remained La Riviere.

lady just throw out the number," remembers a former staffer from CKY. It would be a canard to suggest the young disc jockeys were interested in providing these ladies only with the best in musical entertainment. In this weird and wacky subculture, one particular "groupie" became a celebrity in her own right. The young woman who is remembered by several different names was a regular on the hit line, and a fixture at community clubs whenever a disc jockey and band were in attendance. She travelled with a small dog called "Cochise" and insisted the animal be in the room whenever romantic activity was taking place. An oft-told piece of radio lore concerns a young band member who was nipped by the yappy canine at a most inopportune time, in a most inopportune place.

CKY and CKRC were, in fact, locked in a fierce battle for listeners and advertising revenue. The disc jockeys lived a tenuous existence. To a large degree, rock radio operated on a "what have you done for me lately" mentality. A drop in listening audience or the arrival of a new program

director usually meant a disc jockey was on the road seeking new employment. Stations were not above attempting to steal a big name jock away from his present employer. Being a DJ was a transient business, with top jocks continuously on the move from one station to the other...often the only way they could make a little more money. CKY went through numerous incarnations. "We saw lots of changes," remembers Embree McDermid, a longtime staffer. "There weren't many 25th anniversary parties." A house cleaning could come at any moment.

On a bleak March day in 1964, the Manitoba broadcasting community was shocked with word that Lloyd Moffat had died while vacationing in Hawaii. The head of Moffat Communications, which owned CKY radio, was only 55 years old. His son Randy, 20 years of age, was called upon to take over the company which by now had interests in several radio and television stations across the west. It was a steep learning curve. By the arrival of Canada's Centennial, CKY was no longer a top 40 radio station. Although popular

and influential, it had been a very expensive format to run, particularly when bringing in outside talent. The new CKY was aimed at an adult audience. It featured a homemaking show with Dave Foreman and Hedi Lewis. The new stable of announcers included George Dawes, Dunc Anderson, Ron Andrews, Russ Germain and "Man About Midnight" Jim Coghill. The programming was soft, smooth and far removed from what young Winnipeggers had been used to hearing.

While CKY-AM was now catering to a more mature audience, a strange "flower power" programming concept was developing on the FM side. The mellow sounds synonymous with FM radio gave way on the weekends to what came to be known as "Now Flower." Some called it "hippie radio," as the station offered up album rock and alternative music never before heard on radio airwaves. The cuts could be long and the language strong. Perhaps most remarkable is that program director Herb Brittain ever went for the idea proposed by a young technical operator named Jan Thorsteinson.

Brittain, a veteran musician from the big band era, was nearing retirement. His own band had toured the US and Europe. He once filled in for Rudy Vallee when Vallee was unable to make a show at the Savoy hotel in London. For more than 20 years, he directed the Hudson's Bay Choir. Former CKY engineer Michael Gillespie remembers Brittain using a knife to scratch out album cuts not deemed appropriate for FM. Whether the program director had just lost interest, or was one of the most open-minded individuals in radio, "Now Flower" continued and gained a following over a three-year period when FM programming was in its embryonic stages.

CFRW

By the end of the decade, another Winnipeg radio station had hopped on the rock 'n' roll train. Located at 1470 on the dial, CFRW had been on the air only four years. There was a certain irony in that the new entry into the Winnipeg marketplace was playing the latest hits. Licensed in 1963 under the call letters CJQM, the station's owners pledged "quality" music radio. Among the original shareholders of Winnipeg Radio Ltd. was musician and future head of Rainbow Stage, Jack Shapira, who unleashed a scathing attack on rock radio when making the bid to have the new station approved. "A glorification of the jukebox, low brow programming" were his exact words. Another early investor was "sing and whistle" advocate, John Oliver Blick. Blick had sold CJOB in 1961 to the Griffiths family of Vancouver.

From the outset, CJQM was under-capitalized and a chronic money loser. Blick tried to re-invent it in the style of CJOB, emphasizing all things local and changing the call letters to CFRW...the RW standing for "radio Winnipeg." The strategy paid few dividends. By the late '60s, hip young disc jockeys were brought in, including Mal Faris, Darrell Provost and morning man Duff Roman from Toronto, who had been instrumental in launching the recording career of David Clayton Thomas of Blood Sweat and Tears. CFRW's "Much More Music" was the "new" sound of Winnipeg.

On Tuesday, November 4, 1969, Winnipeggers listening to CFRW had no inclination of what was going on in the Confederation Building on Main Street where the station's studios and offices were located. Late in the afternoon, staff became aware something major was about to come down. At 4:45 pm, a brief announcement was made...Radio Winnipeg Ltd. had declared bankruptcy. The next song was "O Canada"...then dead air. CFRW had gone silent.

It turned out the station was off the air for only a little over twelve hours. By six the next morning, CFRW was back, albeit in a drastically scaled-down version. What happened overnight is not clear, except that a potential White Knight had emerged in the person of an up and coming entrepreneur from Vancouver. Jim Pattison was in the process of building a media empire on the west coast and had been contacted about the troubled radio station in Winnipeg. For much of the next month,

CFRW
BOSS 70 of '70

*36	Share The Land	Guess Who
37	Come To Me	Tommy James & Shondells
38	Rapper	Jaggerz
39	Lola	Kinks
40	Gypsy Women	Brian Hyland
41	El Condor Pasa	Simon & Garfunkel
42	Travelling Band	Creedence Clearwater Revival
43	Vehicle	Ides of March
44	Close To You	Carpenters
45	Make It With You	Bread
46	Cracklin Rosie	Niel Diamond
47	Eli's Coming	Three Dog Night
48	Teach Your Children	Crosby, Stills, Nash & Young
49	Rainy Night In Georgia	Brook Benton
50	Don't Cry Daddy	Elvis Presley
51	He Ain't Heavy, He's My Brother	Hollies
*52	Ivy In Her Eyes	Mongrels
*53	One Tin Soldier	Original Caste
54	Tighter and Tighter	Alive and Kicking
*55	Snowbird	Anne Murray
56	Ain't No Mountain High Enough	Diana Ross
57	Hey There Lonely Girl	Eddie Homman
58	Daughter of Darkness	Tom Jones
59	My Belle Amie	Tea Set
*60	Hey Lawdy Mama	Steppenwolf
*61	Cinnamon Girl	Niel Young
62	Little Green Bag	George Baker Selection
63	The Letter	Joe Cocker
64	Turn Back The Hands of Time	Tyrone Davis
65	Mississippi Queen	Mountain
66	Looking Out My Back Door	Creedence Clearwater Revival
67	25 or 6 to 4	Chicago
*68	Hand Me Down World	Guess Who
69	Riki Tiki Tavi	Donovan
*70	Tobacco Road	The Fifth

CFRW 1470
BOSS
30
Week Ending January 6, 1971

Inside the *CFRW*

BOSS 70 of '70

Johnny McGuinness, J-Jay Jeffrie
Charles P., Bobby Brannigan,
Darell Provost, Dave Harrison,
Mike Rivers, Chuck Morgan
and Jerry Kay

WOULD LIKE TO WISH YOU

"A Super '71"

CFRW 1470

CFRW Boss Radio hit list.
CAVIN BORODY AND GARRY MOIR COLLECTION

CFRW was operated by a bankruptcy trustee while Pattison weighed his options. According to the Vancouver businessman, the station had lost a million dollars since its inception six years earlier and was facing major debts from secured and unsecured creditors. Among those with claims were 22 staff members who had lost wages. Finally Pattison made his offer. One hundred thousand dollars. The bankruptcy trustee accepted.

Pattison stuck with the rock 'n' roll format, embracing the boss radio sound with disc jockeys such as Charles P. Rodney Chandler, Bobby "Boom Boom" Branigan, James (Jim) Millican, Robert J. Buckingham and Chuck Morgan. The new owners had the means to market and sell. The CFRW turn-around was underway. According to one published report, by 1972 the station had net earnings of over $250,000. The Toronto-based CHUM network was looking to expand west. Pattison was reportedly offered $2.5 million for his Winnipeg radio station. To no one's surprise he accepted...an excellent return on a $100,000 dollar investment. There was big money in rock radio.

Can-Con

The arrival of a balding law professor as leader of the Liberal Party and prime minister marked yet another twist in radio's journey. Pierre Trudeau became the first Canadian political leader to effectively define himself through television. Women thought he was sexy, and audiences screamed as they might at a rock concert. Trudeaumania swept the land and the Liberals swept to power with a massive majority in the 1968 election. In the midst of this, another Pierre was appointed to a powerful new agency set up to regulate broadcasting in Canada. Pierre Juneau, a long time colleague of Trudeau in Quebec, had been given the job as chairman of the Canadian Radio Television Commission. The CRTC had been formed as the result of a new Broadcasting Act, replacing the Board of Broadcast Governors. The Commission was given considerably more power than its predecessor and it was soon evident Juneau would be an activist chairman.

The role of broadcasting as a nation builder, and concern over American cultural influence, had been constant themes for more than four decades. Juneau and the Liberals took the debate to a new level in February of 1970 with the announcement that, in future, both radio and television stations would have to meet stringent Canadian content requirements. For AM radio, 30 percent of the music played would have to be Canadian, as defined by the Commission. The policy would make Juneau a hero or villain, depending on one's perspective. Private broadcasters, for the most part, were bitterly opposed to the concept, claiming there was not enough quality Canadian music to meet the new quotas. An even stronger argument was that Can-Con represented gross government intervention in the marketplace, undermining freedom of choice. Some radio stations took to irreverently describing Canadian songs as "beavers," and a few even cut down on

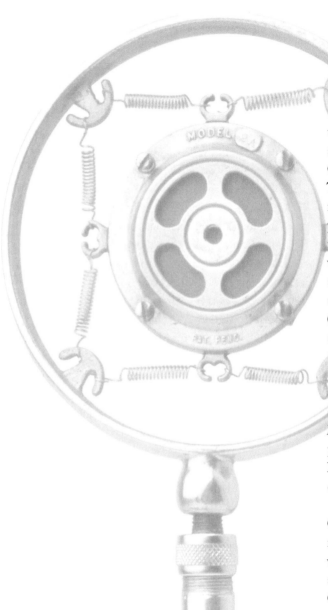

the length of certain songs. Intransigence and perceived arrogance on the part of the Commission further exacerbated relations. The Commission's preoccupation with the minutia of everyday programming was particularly galling. Stations were required to keep detailed records of everything that went on the air. "They would want to know about a weather report, how long it was, and when it ran. There were people there (at the Commission) who had no idea how a radio station operated," recalls one former station manager.

The government agency had most of the cards and all the power. Can-Con prevailed, and over the years would be expanded. Manitoba radio stations had done much to promote and develop local musical talent. In the future, they would be expected to do even more.

Amid the hubbub of rock 'n' roll, Canadian content and the nation's centennial celebrations, the real future of radio was quietly beginning to unfold in studios at 930 Portage Avenue, the new home of CJOB. General manager Rory Maclennan

and the station's west coast owner Western Broadcasting were turning their attention to FM. In 1965, CJOB FM broke new ground, becoming the first FM station in Canada to opt for a country music format. The move represented a dramatic break with conventional wisdom that FM was the exclusive domain for classical or so called "beautiful music." "Everybody was doing classical music and audience penetration was about two percent of the population. If you were lucky you might have 20 or 30 listeners," recalls Peter Grant, CJOB FM's first full-time program director. With the switch, the station suddenly had an exclusive and potentially huge audience, although the problem remained that many radios still had no FM band.

The format change, however, was but the beginning of CJOB's FM innovation. Any on-air personality picking up a local newspaper on October 11, 1968, had ample reason for concern. Eaton's department store was running large advertisements urging shoppers to visit the sixth floor to see "the radio station of tomorrow."

Automation had arrived. CJOB FM would be the first radio station in Canada to test it out. According to newspaper accounts, the station was run "by a giant computer that plays music and radio commercials and performs many of the jobs of an on-air disc jockey. Some day all radio stations will have this system."

The computer was indeed a giant, well over six feet high and taking up the wall of a sizable bathroom. It even had a name... STAN. Although purchased from an American manufacturer, CJOB engineer Neil East completely reprogrammed the machine to suit the station's requirements even making a change that allowed the announcer's voice to be heard over the instrumental version of a song and be stopped just before the lyrics began. For the next eight years, CJOB FM was, for all intents and purposes, an automated jukebox.

"We only had three people on staff," says Grant. "It made us profitable for the first time." STAN, however, did have his drawbacks. "What we missed out on was the interaction between audience and announcers...the contests, the fun, the requests...we couldn't do requests. Some (staff) left because they didn't believe in that kind of programming."

Although it would take several decades, each of these innovations would become commonplace. With the development of more sophisticated digital technology, voice tracking and automation became standard practise. As FM steadily grew in popularity every station adopted a narrowly focused format catering to specific musical tastes. Future on air personalities like Tom McGouran, Larry Updike, "Brother" Jake Edwards, Tom Milroy, Buster Beau Dean (born Wolfgang Fritzsche) and many more would develop new sounds and new formats on the FM band. Even venerable morning man Don Percy would finish out his career on FM. In the words of one veteran broadcaster, "FM became the domain of the rockers. AM was relegated to the talkers."

CHAPTER TWELVE

Yakety Yak

Since its inception, radio had been a source of information. By the 1960s, the medium was no longer a one-way street. Broadcasters were realizing that listeners had much to contribute, which could make for some very interesting programming. Broadcast journalism was by now well established. Even the Winnipeg Press Club, long the domain of print journalists, had voted in 1957 to allow broadcasters to become members. The spirited debate that led to the vote had pitted brothers, two of the city's most prominent media personalities, against each other. Eric Wells of the *Winnipeg Tribune* was against the idea. Brother Jack Wells was all for it.

But it was television, not newspapers, which posed a greater threat to radio broadcasters. In November of 1960, a second television station went on the air in Winnipeg. Privately-owned CJAY was filled with former radio broadcasters, including Stewart Macpherson, Jack Wells, Peter Jackson and Ed McCrea. Television viewing was growing exponentially. Watching a supper hour newscast was becoming part of a routine for many Manitobans. Events like the Cuban missile crisis, the Kennedy assassination, early morning space launches and the implosion of the Diefenbaker government made for dramatic television viewing. Mother Nature, however, would soon step in to demonstrate yet again the importance of radio as an information medium.

Just before 7 am on March 4, 1966, Winnipeg Mayor Stephen Juba was awakened by the telephone ringing. Although still groggy at that early hour, he immediately heard the sound of strong winds lashing against the walls of his William Avenue residence. The call was from CJOB news director Steve Halinda, wondering about the city's plans to deal with a blizzard that had hit the city full force. Behind the wheel of his Cadillac, the mayor plowed his way to city hall which, over

Opposite: Getting right down to business. Prime Minister Pierre Trudeau appears on the Peter Warren Show. RORY MACLENNAN FAMILY

the next 24 hours, became an emergency control centre.

By mid-morning, visibility was near zero, with snow drifts blocking many city streets. While a surprising number of people did made it to work and even downtown to shop, it was soon evident this was no ordinary storm.

Radio once again discarded any semblance of regular programming. CBW became the official civil defence emergency station. CJOB opened the phone lines and became a storm coverage centre. Other stations scrambled to provide the latest storm information. At 10:30, the mayor was on the air urging Winnipeggers to stay inside. Just after 11am, the transit system was shut down. Police and emergency vehicles were getting stuck. Hospitals were running low on supplies. By 1:30, with the city virtually at a standstill, city officials took to the airwaves once again with an emergency appeal for any vehicle capable of travelling in the storm. Hundreds of people stranded downtown spent the night sleeping at Eaton's, the Hudson's Bay department store or other locations.

Some broadcasters made gargantuan efforts just to get to work. Porky Charbonneau, back working at CKY, trudged from the Paddock Restaurant at Polo Park to the radio station at 432 Portage Avenue. CKRC's Harry Taylor walked from his home in Windsor Park to the *Free Press* building on Carlton Street. Regular work hours were forgotten and very few broadcasters made it home that night. The *Free Press* did publish that day, but was unable to get the newspapers delivered. CKRC's Bob Washington took to reading the paper on the air. (For Washington, such an activity was "old hat", as one of CKRC's most popular programs had Wash and his colleague, creative writer Tom Ashmore reading the *Free Press* comics every Sunday morning.)

As the storm intensified, radio's role became ever more vital. "The public leaned heavily on the broadcast media," reported the *Free Press* the next day. Through radio, emergency crews or other citizens were directed to seemingly endless problems created by the storm. Given the height of the snow drifts, a number of elderly people were trapped in their homes. Radio put out an appeal for food for people stranded at work, and directed emergency crews that faced a long night ahead. One station put a doctor on the air to explain how to deliver a baby at home.

There were calls about lack of heat due to broken furnaces, hospitals running low on milk, missing pets and loved ones unaccounted for. The day after the storm, the newspaper reported a story about a woman on Simcoe Street who had phoned a radio station seeking help for a small boy stuck in a snow drift. "The woman said she was crippled and couldn't go to the boy's aid." The lad was rescued. It is not a stretch to say that radio was a lifesaver during that wild weekend.

Newsrooms

Through a combination of regulation and commitment to community service, all radio stations maintained newsrooms. Although small by newspaper standards,

CKY News team: Frank Roberts, Bill Grogan, and Vic Edwards. RICK WHITEFORD

the local radio newsrooms made considerable effort to gather their own material. Every station was a member of the legislative press gallery. City hall, metro council and even school board meetings were part of the regular news beat. As CKY and CKRC were building their programming around rock 'n' roll, their newsrooms were in vigorous competition with CJOB in covering the news of the day. At CKRC, Jim Farrell and Lee Sage provided coverage of breaking news. The venerable Ev Dutton, by now the dean of broadcast journalism in western Canada, was a fixture at the Manitoba legislature.

CKY news director Bill Trebilcoe had become something of a multimedia star. In addition to his work at the radio station, he had his own column in the *Winnipeg Free Press* and was a regular panellist on a CJAY television program called "20 Questions." Six-foot-five "Stretch" Trebilcoe even found time for a romantic relationship with fellow panellist Edna "Rassy" Ragland. The single mom, known for her acerbic tongue, had plenty to deal with herself, managing the up

and coming music career of her teenage son Neil Young.

In its rock 'n' roll days, CKY's news was fast-paced, short and punchy. For a time, newscasts were moved to five minutes to the hour so that the station could roll music while other broadcasters were airing news. Sound and performance were key

ingredients of the programming formula. Whether it was Frank Roberts reporting from the Public Safety building, or Vic Edwards reading a newscast, there was a defined style that was unique to the station. Another big news voice, picked up in the mid-'60s, was John Pierce, who would ultimately replace Trebilcoe as news director.

R. M. MacLENNAN
Station Manager
CJOB-CJOB-FM

Canada's Centennial marks the twenty-first year of broadcasting by CJOB. A twenty-first Birthday is a milestone of maturity, and 'OB ranks with the mature and responsible stations of Canada.

"Working for Winnipeg" — a promise to the Community, was instituted in 1946 and is still the byword of CJOB's dedicated staff today.

A thoughtful review of Canada's growth in the past one hundred years reveals the great progress in Communications — and in particular the growth and development of Radio as a vital medium. CJOB stands proudly with the Radio Industry of Canada.

CLIFF GARDNER
Program Director
CJOB-CJOB-FM

Canada's birthday has given us the opportunity to add new ingredients to the 'OB fare of service and entertainment. A distinctive series of programs bringing to Winnipeg and Manitoba the excitement and pleasure of Centennial, began a few moments after this great year started.

'OB has been described by many over the years as "the station where something is always happening". In 1967, a year of action, CJOB and its listeners will be very much part of the action.

RED ALIX

Fresh every morning when the clock says WAKE UP WINNIPEG. Special attention for those needing cheering up and turning on. Red is the first to know Winnipeg's feelings on BEEFS AND BOUQUETS and the BEELINE.

GEORGE McCLOY

Host of the most popular housewives program in Winnipeg, LADIES CHOICE. Over 25,000 ladies are members. Sunday mornings George sends greetings to "shut-ins" all over Manitoba on THE SHUT-INS PROGRAM.

GARRY ROBERTSON

Garry's afternoon HOUSE PARTY is the friendliest program in town. Anything can happen, and it happens in a most easygoing manner. Special and surprise guests make life interesting for the host and you.

ALLEN WILLOUGHBY

To help the commuter as he wends his way home, and to keep him in touch with the world, Allen and a cast of characters live it up on the HOMEWARD HUSTLE. They make any journey more pleasant.

THE MUSIC ROOM

The perfect match for the evening hours . . . THE MUSIC ROOM. There's lots more music inside and the door is open to anyone with the right combination (just dial 6 and 8 on your radio).

BILL EASTON

A wide awake NIGHT OWL who keeps things going for the special brand of people who stay awake and work while the rest of the world sleeps. Bill is president of the IN-SOMNIAC CLUB.

Steve Halinda

Dudley Paterson

Ron James

Bob Beaton

Don Lynn

CJOB BROADCAST NEWS

News Manager, Steve Halinda, directs a staff of responsible newsmen who personally cover the miles of Metro and Manitoba.

Now, through the facilities of NBC NEWS and its 800 reporters stationed all over the globe, 'OB newsmen have the world at their fingertips. Every day, CJOB Broadcast News covers the world better.

NEWS TRAVELS FAST ON CJOB

There was no disputing, however, that CJOB was Winnipeg's "information station." Jack Blick's assessment when he banned rock 'n roll had largely been correct. As other stations competed for a young audience, CJOB was left with a large pool of affluent listeners from which to draw. News directors Allan Bready, and later Steve Halinda, built strong newsrooms. A new hire from Dauphin named Bob Beaton became CJOB's voice of the Manitoba legislature. Ken McCreath would go on to become a national reporter for CBC radio, and another newcomer, Roger Currie, would eventually host the CJOB morning show.

'OB took its coverage to a new level in the early 1960s with "Beacon Weekends." In the simplest terms, the station committed itself to local coverage all weekend long to get people to the cottage, the beach or wherever they might be going. The CJOB traffic cruiser would be on the highways Friday afternoons and Sunday evenings as Winnipeggers made their way into and out of the city. Weather reports from resort areas were regularly updated. Newscasts ran every hour on the hour. "It turned out to be a very, very successful move," says 1960's CJOB staffer Bill Stewart, who was hired to travel around the city doing interviews about weekend activities. "In those days, 'OB was still doing block programming on Sundays and still would not accept individual commercial announcements...you could sponsor a program but you couldn't buy an ad." "Beacon Weekends" changed all that, providing the station with a new source of revenue.

CJOB's focus on weekend coverage helped set it apart from other stations. "Sunday morning was one of the most important days of the week for us," remembers former program director and general manager John Cochrane. "Radio traditionally throws it away. To me it didn't make a damned bit of sense. That's when everyone is home."

In addition to local coverage, CJOB had purchased the NBC broadcast news service, which at that point claimed to have "800 reporters stationed all over the globe." "Every day," chimed one promotional brochure, "CJOB Broadcast News covers the world."

In March 1966, however, it was Winnipeg radio reporters being heard around the world, following the biggest gold robbery in Canadian history. No Hollywood writer could have come up with a script more compelling. Two men arrived at the airport, dressed as Air Canada employees. They stole an Air Canada van, drove it to an aircraft that had just landed, helped the workers unload almost $400,000 worth of gold bricks into their vehicle, then drove to a waiting getaway car. The heist was masterminded by an "affable" criminal named Ken Leishman. Fate intervened, as the March 4 storm prevented Leishman from getting the gold out of town, and he and his four accomplices were arrested a week later. Before the year was out, Leishman had escaped and been recaptured, not once but twice.

Former CBC radio producer, Heather Robertson, penned a book about the great Winnipeg gold robbery. In it, she describes how Leishman was glued to CJOB the night

of the robbery to determine how quickly authorities had noticed the missing gold. The sheer audacity of the heist captured the imagination of Winnipeggers. The event was the talk of the town, with the chattering reaching a frenzy when a reward was offered. Anyone with information leading to the capture of the robbers and return of the stolen goods could be eligible for a reward of 10 percent of the value of the gold. "Everyone in Winnipeg turned detective," wrote Robertson. "All the paranoiac fantasies of a peaceful prairie population burst like a cloud-burst over the open line radio shows."

The Pastor

The open line radio show was, in fact, a relatively new programming concept for Manitobans. The earliest local talk show was not about current events, but religion. "Ask the Pastor" first aired on CKY in 1952. Hosted by Pastor H.H. Egler of the First Lutheran Church on Maryland St. in Winnipeg, the show developed a dedicated following and, in fact, did many of the things that became standard practise on future call-in programming.

Every Sunday at 10 pm, Egler would trudge up the stairs of the CKY building on Main Street. At 10:30, host and technical operator Don Kirton would voice the standard opening. "Do you have a problem? Ask the pastor."

"In moments," recalled Kirton, "the phone lines would be loaded with anxious callers. A father would call in asking why he could no longer communicate with his children, an atheist would call just to argue about religion, and occasionally a call from a troubled teenager … 'Pastor Egler, I'm 15, my boyfriend is 16, we want to get married because I'm pregnant.'"

The job also required a sense of humour, as over the years there was no shortage of prank calls. On one occasion, a listener called about a female companion no longer responding to his touch the way she once had. The "friend" turned out to be his milk cow. "We had a delay button," recalls Kirton, "but I didn't know how to use it."

The pastor, however, was deeply committed to his radio ministry, which went far beyond the 90 minutes he spent in the studio. Kirton notes "he found time to allow part of his regular day for special counselling for those who required more help than a telephone answer. There were many special cases. He would assist in helping people find proper medical attention or legal advice."

"I tried to be a good shepherd," remembered Egler, in an interview years after he left Winnipeg. "I helped people who tried to commit suicide and had them on for all sorts of reasons. The program was really something that helped all sorts of people."

In its rock 'n' roll heyday, CKY ran a syndicated open line program hosted by American Joe Pyne. The abrasive Pyne, who worked in Montreal for a time, thrived on controversy. His argumentative programming style became a model for generations of future talk show hosts, from Jack Webster in Vancouver to Don Imus in New York. "Go ahead, shoot your mouth off," Pyne would challenge guests and callers. On his television program, Pyne once accused a guest of "lying in your teeth… if they are yours."

With no local content, the Joe Pyne show had a limited shelf life. The first local current events talk show was hosted by Bill Trebilcoe on CKY. "There's nothing we won't talk about," boasted the show's promotional material. Trebilcoe was a natural for open line programming. Outgoing and articulate, he was an accomplished and much sought after guest speaker. As an active member of the Winnipeg Press Club, he was well connected to the city's movers and shakers. For years, he hosted the Press Club's annual Beer and Skits presentation… an irreverent theatrical production satirizing local newsmakers.

Most of all, Trebilcoe was an experienced and committed journalist who was prepared to listen to all sides of an issue. On any given day, listeners might hear an influential cabinet minister…or Bertha Rand, an eccentric cat lover who never turned away a stray feline. From time to time, Trebilcoe's name would pop up in the Manitoba legislature as politicians would refer to something heard on the program to buttress their own arguments. Like Pastor Egler before him, he would spend off-air hours trying to assist some of the listeners who had called the program. Trebilcoe's passing in 1971, after open heart surgery, shocked his listeners. A single line in his obituary best summed up his success as an open line host. "To thousands of Manitobans, Mr. Trebilcoe was recognized as the province's unofficial ombudsman."

The success and ratings of the "Bill Trebilcoe By-Line" were not lost on management at rival CJOB. Winnipeg's "information station" was not about to be beaten by CKY, and the decision was made that CJOB would have its own open line show. The challenge was to find a host. Not just anyone could carry a three hour a day talk show, five days a week. There were very few broadcasters in the country with open line experience. Program director Cliff Gardner and general manager Rorie Maclennan cast

CKY talk show host Bill Trebilcoe at Winnipeg news event.
Also seen in photo holding microphone is CJOB's Bob Beaton.
WINNIPEG PRESS CLUB COLLECTION

their eyes west to CKX in Brandon. The news director at the station was a 28-year-old named John Harvard. The farm boy from Glenboro had worked in the CJOB newsroom for five years, beginning in 1960, and had developed a reputation as a hard-nosed journalist.

On Canada's 100th birthday, July 1, 1967, CJOB launched "The John Harvard Show." The job was high profile and brutally demanding. "You got nothing (in terms of resources)," recalled Harvard. "You're your own researcher, your own producer, your own host, your own writer. I was in the station most mornings by 6:30 and I don't think I ever got out before five o'clock in the afternoon and often back in the evening. It was so challenging. You could have a great show, the phones ringing off the wall. You would really feel good the way it went. Then you'd get back to the office at 11:30 and you'd look up at the board for tomorrow and there wasn't a damn thing there. You do it all over again."

The hard work paid off. In two years, the "John Harvard Show" had overtaken CKY as the most listened-to talk show in the city. The testament to the program's influence came the night after the election of Manitoba's first New Democratic Party government. Premier-elect Ed Schreyer appeared on a special edition of Harvard's program to talk directly to the people about what a social democratic government might do.

On air, Harvard could be gruff, grouchy, opinionated and ready to challenge news-makers on the issues of the day. In the late '60s, there was no shortage of hot button topics. The emerging women's movement, drug use, draft dodgers, and Trudeaumania all provided grist for the mill. Harvard once framed a program with the question "Is your daughter a hippie? What makes a real hippie? What happens at a love-in?"

For a talk show host, finding a topic that will generate listener interest can be like mining for gold. Important as an issue might be, there are days when it seems nothing can stir audience attention. Then suddenly, sometimes without warning, the host hits pay dirt. Every telephone line into the studio is blinking...everyone, it seems, wants to be on the radio. Such was the case in late December, 1969.

In keeping with routine, John Harvard arrived at CJOB before 7 am on Monday, December 22. He was always apprehensive about Mondays. Christmas was just around the corner, and on Mondays people never seemed keen on talking. This particularly Monday, however, would be different.

The previous Saturday night, during a CBC network television program, the newly-elected NDP government had extended an invitation to former Beatle John Lennon to visit Manitoba. A rock festival was to be part of the province's 1970 Centennial activities and the Manitoba Centennial Corporation knew Lennon would be a huge draw. To everyone's surprise, Lennon, without hesitation, promised to "be there."

Lennon and partner Yoko Ono had been spending a good deal of time in Canada as part of their "give peace a chance" initiative, including their infamous bed-in at Montreal's Queen Elizabeth hotel. No one symbolized the generation gap more than the counter-culture couple. To suggest Lennon was a divisive figure is an understatement. Always ready to stir the pot, Harvard came out four-square against the visit. When his show went on the air at nine, he had lined up the NDP MLA for Elmwood, Russell Doern, the man who had extended the invitation to Lennon on Saturday night television. It was soon evident no one on the Centennial planning committee had made any preparations for such a quick and positive response from the rebellious Englishman. According to Doern, Harvard went on the attack immediately, describing Lennon as an "immoral long-haired hippie who had impregnated his wife before they were married."

Then came the callers. "We don't want this hairy man here," raged one female listener whose comments reflected many that morning. "He will cause only trouble and we have enough trouble as it is. This man allowed himself to be photographed in the nude and had the nerve to put the picture on the back of a record album. Any man who would do that is not a decent man."

The war of words between Lennon's supporters and detractors was underway, and talk radio was the battlefield. "It was probably the most vicious outpouring of hatred in the city's history," wrote Doern in his book *Wednesdays are Cabinet Days.* "For three days, leather-lunged hotline housewives screamed over the airwaves. It was frightening."

By the following Wednesday, CKY open line host Jerry Haslam, who had replaced an ailing Bill Trebilcoe, was so sick and tired of the vitriol, he refused any more calls on the topic.

John Lennon never did come to Manitoba. The topic faded away. The entire episode, however, was a case study of how open line radio could take an issue to a different level.

Information Radio

While private stations "duked it out" with talk programming, pop music and sports, CBW radio struggled to find an audience.

Saddled with blocks of network programming of limited appeal, local CBC radio was in need of an identity. That task would fall to program director Ernie Mutimer. A graduate of the Lorne Greene Academy of Broadcasting in Toronto, Mutimer had nearly 20 years experience with CBC radio and television. He and other members of the CBC brain trust seized on the idea of tossing out all music and instead offering a two and a half hour information morning show. While the concept hardly met with overwhelming approval within the CBC, the idea had some merit. The station already had a well-established news operation that included veteran journalists like Herb Nixon, Frank MacGregor, Jake O'Donnell and George Legree. A production unit was formed to develop a full format.

Soldiering forward, CBC management moved the existing morning show, hosted by Lee Major, to the FM band, and on September 15, 1969, "Information Radio" went on the air. The program "is a definite departure from the usual morning fare," declared a *Free Press* review, noting

A LEG FROM LEGS

New York gangster, Jack "Legs" Diamond, was probably never heard of in Winnipeg. Yet for one Winnipeg broadcaster, the name "Legs" Diamond would always elicit a certain chill. As an aspiring journalist, Everell Fletcher "Ev" Dutton had wandered far from his Winnipeg home, taking a job with the *New York Telegram* newspaper. Barely 20 years old, Dutton had been assigned to the crime desk.

On a muggy summer night in the mid 1920s, the newspaper received a tip that police were closing in on a big-time criminal. During the Prohibition era, Jack "Legs" Diamond, also known as "Gentleman Jack," was one of New York City's most notorious gangsters. His control of booze smuggling was known for its violence, including several murders at his "Hotsy Totsy" nightclub. At different points in his career, he was aligned with such notable mobsters as Arnold Rothstein (who conspired to fix the 1919 baseball world series) and Lucky Luciano (considered the father of organized crime in the United States). Although married, Diamond was also known as a ladies' man. On the night in question, his mistake was showing up at a girlfriend's apartment, which police were watching.

Young Ev was ordered by his editor to get the story and a photograph. Arriving at the apartment, he bounded up two flights of stairs. "Just as 'Legs' Diamond was approaching the top of the stairs in the custody of two cops, I stepped in front to take a snap (photograph)," remembered Dutton. Living up to his reputation, "Legs" aimed a foot at the young reporter, catching him squarely and toppling him backwards down the stairs. "I never even got the picture because he kicked before I got the snap."

It was Dutton's good fortune not to be seriously injured. Not only did he have a great story for his newspaper, but a yarn he could tell the rest of his life. After bouncing around several newspaper jobs during the Depression, Dutton landed a position with CJRC (CKRC) radio in 1937, remaining at the station until his retirement in the 1970s. He was one of the city's most respected newsmen, often referred to as the "dean" of broadcast journalist in western Canada.

Manitoba broadcasting executives Rory MacLennan, Elmer Hildebrand, and Roland Couture with a CRTC representative. The Manitoba executives played an influential role in several national broadcasting organizations.
CKSB COLLECTION: LA SOCIETE HISTORIQUE DE SAINT BONIFACE

that existing morning shows consisted of "mostly music and chat with short newscasts on the hour and one main sports report."

Indeed, it was very different. The program offered regular local and national news updates, weather, sportscasts, an agricultural report, interviews, documentaries and commentaries. The original on-air crew included newsreaders Colin Fraser and Ken Dunston; Bob Allison provided regular updates from a mobile news cruiser; Bob Picken and Don Wittman handled sports, with Jim Rae responsible for farm news. There was no format like it in Winnipeg or anywhere in Canada.

The glue that held the program together was host Bill Guest. A native of Sioux Lookout, Ontario, Guest had worked at CKRC for a decade before moving to the CBC. He was already well-known as television's quiz master on the popular high school game program "Reach For the Top." His voice, rich and resonant, coupled with near perfect diction, gave the show an authoritative and polished sound. Guest could segue from one item to the next as smoothly as any disc jockey could slide from one piece of music to another. Recognized for his ad-libbing skills, the reality was he rarely ad-libbed anything. Each day he carried to the studio a small box of ink-stained cards loaded with anecdotes, trivia and assorted minutiae that might fit with an item on "Information Radio." Off air, Guest was witty, had an acerbic tongue and, at times, a penchant for adolescent jokes. Most often, the victim was unsuspecting fellow announcer Jack Turnbull. On at least one occasion when exiting the studio, Guest cut loose with a burst of flatus, leaving the unfortunate Turnbull, just starting his newscast, to suffer the consequences.

Guiding "Information Radio" through those early months was no small undertaking. Private broadcasters griped about the subsidized CBC trying to compete with them. (Until 1974, CBC radio was permitted to run commercials.) Listeners loyal to the previous morning show and missing their music, peppered CBC management with letters of complaint. "I used to get people calling saying 'what have they done to the morning show at CBC'," says Lee Major. Trying to manoeuvre anything new through the bureaucracy of the Corporation could be painstaking. Trade unions were strong, with different unions representing different groups of workers. Job descriptions were clearly defined. Even getting a news story on the air could be cumbersome. A reporter would go out to cover the event. Once written and approved by an editor, a technician was required to handle the recording of the piece and any editing necessary. Once recorded, the report would go to a producer in the studio control room. An announcer in the studio would read the introduction to the story. The producer would then cue a technician who would, in turn, push the proper button to play the report.

With its variety and depth of coverage, the show gained a loyal and, more importantly, growing audience. For years, Ernie Mutimer took delight in telling the story of how one private broadcaster had the issue of "Information Radio" raised in the House of Commons. "They actually brought it up in Parliament...the fact that the CBC radio system actually dared to go after an audience. We did and we got it baby...those ratings were sweet." Some accused the program of being "left leaning," and there were times "Information Radio" would push the envelope, particularly on social issues. One summer in the early 1970s, the program stocked its entire on-air team with women: Agatha Moir as host, Alice Poyser reading news, Barbara Huck reporting on sports, with features provided by future playwright and Member of Parliament, Wendy Lill. Certainly there were women on morning shows before. At CKRC, receptionist Joanne Styles had become an important part of the shtick on the popular "Don Slade show." Prior to Information Radio, however, women had never been in such prominent roles.

Over time, the all-information format spread to noon and afternoon programming. Every CBC AM station across the country eventually adopted information programming in the morning. More than 45 years after it was implemented,

"Information Radio" would still be running on CBC Winnipeg with the program among the top rated shows in the city.

As Manitobans prepared to celebrate the province's centennial in 1970, the CBC had only just begun its campaign to become a greater force in the local marketplace. Plans were underway for a beefed-up supper hour news and current events program on CBC television. The program would be called "24 Hours." On radio, a new talk show called "Questionnaire" was in the making, which would run just after the noon hour farm broadcast. Very quietly, feelers went out early in the summer to two of Winnipeg's best-known private broadcasters. In early August, the CBC sent shock waves through the industry with word that talk show veterans Jerry Haslam and John Harvard had been lured away from CKY and CJOB to host the new programs.

Private broadcasters were incensed. "It isn't the CBC's position to use public money to put on shows that private companies are prepared to put on the air," griped CKY President Randy Moffat. The fiercest opposition, though, came from within the CBC itself. The jobs for which Harvard and Haslam had been hired were never advertised, and the powerful unions within the corporation took this as a direct challenge. Jack Turnbull, who headed the announcers' union blustered and cursed. "This is a very serious grievance," he seethed in a newspaper interview. From the union's perspective, the hirings were a blatant violation of their collective agreement, which stated "announcers will have equal opportunities in all fields." On September 10, the issue came to a head when 22 CBC employees, many of them "Information Radio" announcers, walked off the job. The program was kept on the air by management, and the so-called "study session" lasted but a day. Cooler heads prevailed. Harvard and Haslam arrived as planned. The use of contract employees at the CBC had been opened a crack. Talk and information-based programming had taken another step forward.

Gerry Haslam's stay at the CBC was brief before he moved on to the West Coast. Harvard, on the other hand, was part of radio and television programming until 1988 when he jumped into politics and was elected the Liberal Member of Parliament for Winnipeg St. James. He remained an MP until 2004, when he was appointed Lieutenant Governor of Manitoba.

The Action Line

Meanwhile at CJOB, the job of finding a replacement for John Harvard fell to program director John Cochrane and general manager Rory MacLennan. The open-line show had become an important ingredient in the station's success and finding the proper successor was of no small significance. "The talk show was to be done from a purely journalistic point of view," says John Cochrane. "We wanted an experienced journalist." Neither executive could have guessed the candidate they chose would be the most powerful force on the Winnipeg airwaves for the next quarter century.

On the surface, Peter Warren was not an obvious choice. As city editor of the *Winnipeg Tribune*, he had filled in as a guest host a few times, but that was the extent of his radio experience. Born in London,

he had been expelled from school. He had a pronounced English accent and a slight nasal tone that was not naturally appealing. Warren was, however, a tenacious investigative journalist with a flair for showmanship. The former boxer never backed down from a good talk radio scrap. He became the champion of the little guy and was ready to dig deep to correct an injustice. His standard opening on the CJOB "Action Line," "let's get right down to business," became part of the local vernacular.

From the day he was hired in 1971, Warren did get right down to business. Pierre Trudeau appeared on the show, as did a convict doing time at Stony Mountain Penitentiary. Longtime Winnipeg Mayor Steven Juba was almost a regular on the Warren show and even used the program to announce his retirement from politics. Warren fired off a letter to US President Richard Nixon that contained the names of 32 hundred CJOB listeners opposed to an underground bomb test on Amchitka Island in southwest Alaska. Through his "Action Line" program, Warren conducted

a poll on the legalization of marijuana and took up the cause of a Winnipeg woman whose mobster husband had been killed in Montreal, leaving her penniless.

For the next 27 years, Warren kept up a frenetic pace. One could never be quite certain what would happen next on the CJOB "Action Line." Four convicts once gave themselves up on the program. Warren unearthed a homosexual prostitution ring in Winnipeg involving young boys. On another occasion, he tossed a preacher out of the studio.

It was antics like this, along with a grouchy demeanor and a readiness to push the envelope as to what could be discussed on talk radio, that would enchant and also enrage his audience. Listeners would sometimes write six-to-eight page letters skewering him for some perceived wrong. Among the milder critiques:

"Your program on Tuesday morning about women having (sic) birth was the filthiest show on radio....you're a dirty old man. Not a bit decent."

"To Peter Warren...the nosey lunatic."
"You're nothing but a Conservative lapdog."
"Dear Mr. Bleeding Heart Liberal."
"You're a crass, crude, contemptible cad."

On February 5, 1980, Winnipeg police received three phone calls from someone threatening to place a bomb in CJOB unless Peter Warren was removed from the air.

For his part, Warren could give back as well as he got. On his very last "Action Line" program he described one caller as "a snivelling piece of shit."

Overall, admirers far outdistanced detractors. Warren's real appeal came, not from any outrageous programming, but rather from his readiness to help people with everyday problems. "Let me talk to you off the air" was a common phrase on the "Action Line," or "can you send me a 'meemo' about this?"

Warren's files were filled with letters from listeners thanking him for taking on the bureaucracy on their behalf. "This is a thank-you for the help you gave my son with his Autopac, things are being settled," wrote one listener. "Thank you very much for fixing up the mess they made of my husband's unemployment insurance," offered another. "I can't get over what a dynamic worker and champion of the people's causes you are," gushed a third. One of Warren's most popular annual programs involved reading off a list of dormant bank accounts, in the process literally reconnecting people with their own money.

Among the many pieces of mail received was a limerick written by a listener, titled "Ode to Peter." It read in part:

> "Some people think he's wondrous,
>   some others think he stinks.
>   But he really doesn't give a damn
>   what anybody thinks."

Nothing could have been further from the truth. Peter Warren was deeply committed to his craft and it behooved anyone, particularly other members of the news media, to question the value of open line radio. "I'm fed up with so-called 'serious journalists' who put down the radio hotline show," he wrote in a 1974 Maclean's article. "I take my job seriously. I'm a responsible journalist...there isn't any other form of media that can provide a forum so democratic that it puts captains and kings and politicians into direct confrontation with the little guy on the street."

Love him or hate him, people listened in growing numbers. At one point in his career, one out of every three radio listeners in Winnipeg was tuned to the "Action Line." Warren could lay claim to the largest audience share of any talk radio program in a major North American market. The CJOB juggernaut would dominate the local radio market for the next four decades.

News/talk radio would evolve into a format unto itself.

Epilogue

Those Winnipeggers who ventured to Eaton's store in 1910 to witness Dr. De Forest's first wireless demonstration could never have imagined what was to come. Manitoba would ultimately claim well over 100 broadcast signals. FM would be the preferred listening frequency. Radio stations could be operated almost exclusively by a machine. Listeners would be able to hear programming on their telephones and numerous other platforms.

What started as a hobby, mostly among teenage boys, evolved into an established industry. In their first 50 years, Manitoba broadcasters were on the cutting edge of program development, news gathering, technology and community involvement. The groundbreaking efforts of these pioneer broadcasters is evidenced by a long list of radio firsts:

- first licence issued for a commercial radio station
- first election broadcast in Canada
- first publicly-owned radio station in Canada
- first female broadcaster
- first educational broadcasting in Canada
- first Cree language broadcast in Canada
- first radio broadcast of an entire hockey game
- first French language station in western Canada
- first station to provide news "on the hour every hour"
- first FM station in western Canada
- first regular Ukrainian language broadcasting in North America
- first recordings of Neil Young
- first recordings of Burton Cummings and the Deverons
- first station to play the Beatles in North America
- first "information/current events" format in Canada
- first station to broadcast a women's hockey game
- first automated radio station

One cannot begin to name every member of the Manitoba diaspora that would influence broadcasting across Canada, the United States and, in some cases, around the world. A small sampling illustrates how former Manitobans shaped broadcasting. Every early Canadian radio station built on the technical and programming work of Darby Coats. Esse Ljungh and Tommy Tweed helped shape Canadian theatre. The music of Bert Pearl defined a generation. The wartime reporting of Stewart Macpherson touched lives on two continents. Educational broadcasting in numerous countries was modelled on the work of Gertrude McCance. A young CKY hire in the 1940s named Earl Cameron would become known to Canadians as the anchor of the CBC television national news. In the era of rock 'n' roll, J. Robert Wood and Warren Cosford set the standard for programming and production.

Others, such as Cliff Gardner, Jack Wells, Don Wittman, John Cochrane and Elmer Hildebrand never left Manitoba, but their influence on the industry extended far beyond the province's borders.

Impressive as all this might be, radio's ultimate legacy is the impact on its audience; each individual has his or her own story. The grandmother with happy memories of listening to Foster Hewitt's hockey broadcasts. The man whose life was saved after an urgent appeal for blood donors on the radio. The serviceman, thousands of miles from home, reduced to tears when hearing the voice of a loved one. The farmer whose lost horses were returned when word went out over the airwaves. The young woman who backed away from suicide after being directed to seek help by a talk show host. The teenager, listening to rock and roll, inspired to become a world class entertainer.

In its first 50 years, radio touched virtually every Manitoban. It was more than just another media product, a tool to sell merchandise or the latest technological gadget.

Radio was a companion…and a friend.

ACKNOWLEDGMENTS

Having spent over forty years in the local broadcasting industry, I began the process of writing this book under a grand illusion. I was of the opinion I knew something about early radio in Manitoba. Within a week of beginning my research, the bubble had burst. It was evident that, other than a passionate interest in the topic, my knowledge was most limited. Without the co-operation and help of many individuals and organizations, this book would not have been completed.

For anyone interested in broadcast history, a first stop must be the website of the Canadian Communications Foundation. This on-line resource provides a wealth of information about early radio in Canada. La Radio Francaise Saskatchewan site offers a similar service for those interested in the development of French language broadcasting. The people who developed and maintain these resources are owed a debt of gratitude.

Staff at the local history room and micro-media centre at the Winnipeg Millennium Library were invaluable in providing information and copies of back issues of vintage magazines, newspapers and government publications. Very often this served as a starting point for much of the research. It was my good fortune to discover that the Manitoba Provincial Library has maintained a complete set of the Manitoba Telephone System publication *Manitoba Calling*, the radio magazine which ran from 1937 to 1948. Material found in these documents provided the basis for a number of stories that appear in the book. Staff at the Provincial Library were also most helpful in digging up documents about educational broadcasting, including copies of the Department of Education school broadcast magazine *Young Manitoba Listens*. Despite my limited knowledge of the French language, people at the Centre du Patrimoine in St Boniface were enormously accommodating in providing photographs of CKSB radio and copies of *Chante Clair*, the radio magazine published from 1946 to 1953. I would be remiss if I did not mention the work of staff at the University of Manitoba Archives who set up audio equipment in order for me to listen to the "Where Are They Now" recordings which are part of the Peter Warren collection. Other archives staff who also deserve special mention are those at the Mennonite Heritage Centre at Canadian Mennonite University, the Western Canada Pictorial Index at the University of Winnipeg and the S.J. McKee archives at Brandon University. My thanks also go to the volunteers and staff at the Manitoba Electrical Museum and Education Centre in Winnipeg, the Manitoba Amateur Radio Museum in Austin and the Hammond Broadcasting Museum of Radio in Guelph, Ontario.

Recordings done by various radio stations, particularly the CBC and CJOB, proved a wonderful source of anecdotal content. Being able to hear the voices of pioneer broadcasters such as Herb Roberts, Les Garside, Lionel Moore, Ev Dutton and others helped personalize a number of the stories in a way which otherwise could not have been done. Radio stations are to be commended, first for doing these interviews and, secondly, for preserving then.

Having access to the personal CJOB material of Rory MacLennan and the scrapbooks of Herb Roberts was an honor. These men were true broadcast pioneers. Thank you to Marry Jane MacLennan and Randy Roberts for making these resources available.

I also want to thank the many people who gave of their time to be interviewed, answered endless emails and were always available when I had a question. Each of you provided insights into the world of radio that I had never thought of. Thank you to…

Sandy Bazin, (daughter of Digby Hughes CFRY), Dan Brown (CFAM, CKY), Owen Clark (CKY), Jim Coats (son of Darby Coats, CKY), John Cochrane (CKRC, CJOB) , Warren Cosford (CBC, CJOB), Bev Edmondson (CFRY), Vic Edwards (CKY, CFRY), Ross Elliot (CBC), George Gallagar (CKDM), Michael Gillespie (CKY), Peter Grant (CJOB), John Harvard (CJOB, CBC), Elmer Hildebrand (CFAM), George Johns (CKY), Jim Keilback (CKX, CJOB, CKY), Don Kirton (CKY, CJOB), Boyd Kozak (CKRC), Dwight MacAulay (CJRB, CKX, CFAM), Roy MaGuire (CKX, CKRC, CBC), Patrick McDougal (CKY, CKRC), Lee Major (CBC), Rene Maillard (CKDM), Embree McDermid (CKY), Bob McMillan (CKY), Jim McSweeny (CKDM, CKRC, CFAM), Dr. Morris Mott (Brandon University), R.J. "Bob" Picken (CJOB, CBW), Jim Rae (CBC), Carolyn Rickey (CKY, CJOB, CFRW), Bill Stewart (CJOB), Don Taylor (CFAM) and Harry Taylor (CKY ,CKRC).

A most grateful thanks to Great Plains Publications, for taking a chance on a raw rookie. To Ingeborg Boyens, Gregg Shilliday, Catharina de Bakker and Mel Marginet…your creativity, editing and organizational skills made this a better book.

Finally, a very special thank you to my wife Agatha for her endless enthusiasm, encouragement and support. She was my sounding board throughout the entire process, even when I wanted to scrap the whole idea. The book is truly a team effort.

Each of the individuals and organizations mentioned above helped make this publication a reality. However, any errors or deficiencies, of which I hope there are few, are my responsibility alone.

BIBLIOGRAPHY

BOOKS

Bachman, Randy, *Vinyl Tap*, Penguin Books, 2011

Barker, G.F., *Brandon: A City 1881-1961*, Brandon, 1977

Bird, Roger, *Documents of Canadian Broadcasting*, Carleton University Press, Ottawa, 1988

Bocquel, Bernard, *Au Pays de CKSB: 50 Ans de Radio Francaise au Manitoba*, Winnipeg, 1996

Buckingham, Graham A., *Thompson, A City and its People*, Thompson Historical Society, 1986

Bumsted, J.M., *The Manitoba Flood of 1950: An Illustrated History*, Watson and Dwyer Publishers, 1993

CFAM Radio 950: 1957-2007, Golden West Broadcasting, Altona, Manitoba 2007

Davis, Chuck, *Top Dog: A Fifty Year History of BC's Most Listened to Radio Station*, Canada Wide Magazines, Vancouver, 1993

De Forest, Lee, *Father of Radio—An Autobiography of Lee De Forest*, Wilcox and Follet, 1950

Einarson, John, *Shakin All Over The Winnipeg Sixties Rock Scene*, Winnipeg, 1987

Farrell, Allen, *The CHUM Story*, Stoddart Publishing, Toronto, 2001

Fong-Torres, Ben, *The Hits Just Keep on Coming: The History of Top 40 Radio*, Miller Freeman Books, San Francisco, 1998

Gray, James H., *The Winter Years*, MacMillan of Canada, Toronto, 1996

Gordon, George N. and Falk, Irving A., *On the Spot Reporting: Radio Records History*, Julian Messner, New York, 1967

Hallson, Richard, *Out of the Darkness*, R. Hallson, Winnipeg, 2011

Hedman, Valerie; Yauck, Loretta; Henderson, Joyce, *Flin Flon*, Flin Flon Historical Society, 1974

Hodgkinson, Brian, *Spitfire Down*, Penbura Press, 2000.

Kitchen, Paul. *Win, Tie or Wrangle: The Inside Story of the Old Ottawa Senators*, Penumbra Press, Manotick, Ontario, 2008

Lambert, Richard, *School Broadcasting in Canada*, University of Toronto Press, 1963

Letkeman, Peter. *The Ben Horch Story*, Old Oak Publishing, Winnipeg, 2007

Macpherson, Stewart, *The Mike and I*, Home and Van Thal, London, 1948

McDonough, Jimmy, *Shakey: Neil Young's Biography*, Vintage Canada, 2003

McFarlane, Brian, *Proud Past, Bright Future: One Hundred Years of Canadian Women's Hockey*, Stoddart, Toronto, 1995

McNeil, Bill and Morris, Wolf, *The Birth of Radio in Canada*, Doubleday Canada, Toronto, 1982

Metcalfe, William H., *The View From Thirty*, W. H. Metcalfe, Winnipeg, 1984

Mindess, Wilfred E., *Farblonget in the Wilds of North Winnipeg*, Self-Published, 2005

Moir, Agatha, *CBC Manitoba: The Sound of Our Time*, CBC Winnipeg, 1988

Mott, Morris and Allardyce, John, *Curling Capital: Winnipeg and the Roarin Game 1876-1988*, University of Manitoba Press, 1989

Murray, Robert P., *The Early Development of Radio in Canada 1901-1930*, Sonoran Publishing, Chandler, Arizona, 2005

Nash, Knowlton, *The Microphone Wars*, McClelland and Stewart, Toronto, 1994

Nash, Knowlton, *The Swashbucklers*, McClelland and Stewart, Toronto, 2001

Ormand, Raby, *Radio's First Voice: The Story of Reginald Fessenden*, Macmillan of Canada, Toronto, 1970

Peers, Frank W., *The Politics of Canadian Broadcasting 1920-1951*, University of Toronto Press, 1973

Powley, A.E., *Broadcast from the Front: Canadian Radio Overseas in the Second World War*, Hakkert, Toronto, 1975

Roberts, Ron-Forbes, *One Long Tune: The Life and Music of Lenny Breau*, University of North Texas Press, 2006

Robertson, Heather, *The Flying Bandit*, James Lorimer & Company, Toronto, 1980

Roberston, John, *High Times with Stewart MacPherson*, Prairie Publishing, Winnipeg, 1980

Roberston, Lloyd, *The Kind of Life It's Been*, Harper Collins, Toronto, 2012

Stewart, Sandy, *From Coast to Coast– A Pictorial History of Radio in Canada*, CBC Enterprises, 1985

Watson, Franceene, Andy De Jarlis. *Master of Metis Melodies*, Franceene Watson, Victoria, 2002

Weir, Austin E., *The Struggle for National Broadcasting in Canada*, McClelland and Stewart, Toronto, 1965

Wood, Chris, *Live to Air-The Craig Broadcasting Story*, Douglas and McIntyre, 2000

Vien, Russel, *Radio Francaise dans L'Ouest*, Hurtubise, Montreal, 1977

Vipond, Mary, *Listening In: The First Decade in Canadian Broadcasting 1922-32*, McGill-Queens University Press, 1992

ARTICLES

"Advice to Private Broadcasters: Stop Shouting-Talk Facts," Editorial, *Maclean's*, Nov. 24, 1956

Callwood, June, "The Not So Happy Gang," *Maclean's*, Feb.1, 1950

Chante Clair, CKSB radio publication, 1946-1953, Centre du Patrimoine, St. Boniface

Fraser, Blair, "The Vast and Turbulent Empire of the Siftons," *Maclean's*, Dec. 5, 1959

Frayne, Trent, "Winnipeg's Maverick of the Sports Mike," *Maclean's*, Aug. 15, 1959

Goldstein, Ken, "How Winnipeg Invented the Media," *Manitoba History*, Fall 2012

Guthrie, Tyrone, "The Theatre and I," *Maclean's*, Dec. 5, 1959

Harrison, Therasa, "Rory MacLennan: A Radio Pioneer," *Mid Canada Commerce*, September 1986

Johnson, William, "The Only Game in Town," *Sports Illustrated*, February 16, 1970

"Let's Dig Up Those Reds, Dr. McCann, But Don't Muzzle the CBC," Editorial, *Maclean's*, Sept.29, 1956

"125 Years of the Winnipeg Press Club," *Manitoba History*, Fall Issue, 2012 No. 70

Moon, Barbara, "Radio's Future," *Maclean's*, April 27, 1957

Reynolds, George F., "Early Wireless Radio in Manitoba 1909-1924," *Manitoba Historical Society Transactions Series* 3, Number 35, 1978-79

Vipond, Mary, "CKY Winnipeg in the 1920's: Canada's Only Experiment in Government Monopoly Broadcasting" *Manitoba Historical Society*, Number 12, Autumn 1986

Vipond, Mary, "Public Service Broadcasting and Winnipeg Listeners in the 1930's," *Manitoba History*, Volume 27, 2008

Wiebe, Jeremy Robert. "A Different Kind of Radio Station: Radio Southern Manitoba and the Reformulation of Mennonite Identity: 1957-1977," Masters Thesis, University of Manitoba, 2009

Young, Bob, "My Brother the Folk Singer," *Maclean's*, May 1971

PAPERS AND ARCHIVE DOCUMENTS

Abram J. Thiessen Fond: Mennonite Heritage Centre, Canadian Mennonite University

CKSB Fond: Centre du Patrimoine, Franco Manitoban Cultural Centre

Herb Roberts Scrapbook and Papers, (privately held by family)

Lionel Moore Fond: Scrapbook and Papers, University of Manitoba, Elizabeth Dafoe Library

Peter Warren Fond: Recordings and Papers, University of Manitoba, Elizabeth Dafoe Library Rorie MacLennan Papers, (privately held by family).

Theodore E. "Ted" Friesen Fond: CFAM papers, Mennonite Heritage Centre, Canadian Mennonite University

Dan Wood, Scrapbook and papers, donated to CBC, Manitoba

INDEX

Aird Commssion, 38-40
Alix, "Red," 127
Allan, Chad, 149
Allen Theatre, 19
Anderson, Dunc, 158
Andrews, Ron, 158
"Ask the Pastor," 170
Aune, John, 102

Bachman, Randy, 154
Balcan, George, 105
Barker, Howard, 102
Barkley, Brian, 102
Barkman, Dennis, 104, 106
Basaraba, Bernie, 99
Baudouin, Father Maurice, 78
Beacon Weekends, 99
Beaton, Bob, 169, 172
Beaver Club, 60
Bennett, R.B., 39
Benson, Tom, 61 65,
Bird Lady, 119
Blick, John Oliver, 70-77, 90, 130, 146, 147,
    159, 169
Blizzard 1966, 165-166
Board of Broadcast Governors, 106, 131, 161
Bowman, Bob, 57

Bracken, John, 19, 23, 27, 31, 33, 113
Bradburn, Bob, 149, 150-151
Branigan, "Boom Boom" Bobby, 161
Bready, Allan, 76, 169
Breau, Betty (Cody), 127-129
Breau, Hal (Lone Pine), 127-129
Breau, Lenny (Lone Pine Jr.), 127, 147
Bridgman, "Monty" J.M., 49,
Brittain, Herb, 158-159
Broadcasting Act, 131, 161
Brown, Margaret, 115
Buckingham, Robert J., 161
Burchell, Maurice, 86, 90, 123-124
Burlingham, Daryl, 149-150
Burns, Bob, 156

Cameron, Earl, 65, 182
Campbell, Douglas, 90, 104
Canadian Broadcasting Corporation CBC:
    Broadcast Regulator, 129-131; early
    programming, 44-45; FM radio, 77-109;
    formation, 41-43; Information Radio,
    174-178; unions, 177-178
Canadian Central Wireless Club, 14
Canadian Content Regulations, 161-162
Canadian Radio Broadcasting Commission, 39,
    40, 41, 43, 47,78
Canadian Radio League, 39
Canadian Radio and Television Commission, 7,
    131, 161,

Capital Theatre, 19
Carman tower and transmitter, 92-95
Carrier, Russ, 65
Carson, Jack, 92
CFAM, 103-111
CFAR, 47-50
Charbonneau, "Porky" Gene, 126-127, 146, 166
CHFC, 50
CHSM Steinbach, 106
CHTM, 50
CJAR, 50
CJNC, 16-17
CJOB: bans rock music, 147-148; early program-
    ming, 73-75; formation, 72; newsroom, 75-76,
    169; talk programming, 173-174, 179-180
CJOB FM, 77, 162-163
CJQM, 159
CJRB, 141
CJRC, 40-47, 55, 59, 62, 69, 138, 175
CJZC, 16, 18
CKDM, 97-99
CKRC: description of station, 73; morning
    shows, 124-127; name change, 69; newsroom,
    167-175; rock format, 150-154; sports
    coverage, 133-135
CKSB, 77-81
CKX: formation, 33-35; private ownership, 83-85
CKY (MTS station): formation, 22; early
    programming, 23-27; sold to CBC (becomes
    CBW): 82-83, 86

CKY (private station): early programming, 126-128; formation, 86-87; newsroom and talk show, 170-171; rock format, 145-156
CKY FM, 158-159
Clark, Owen, 127
CNRW, 28-30
Coats, Darby, 18, 24-26, 31, 38, 42, 65, 119, 182
Cochrane, John, 124-125, 169, 179, 182
Coghill, Jim, 158
Cohen, Albert, 129
Cook, Chuck, 76-77,
Corrie, Dennis, 127, 149, 156, 157
Cosford, Warren, 129, 150-151, 182
Couture, Roland, 80, 176
Craig, John, 82-85
Criterion Athletic Club, 143
Cummings, Burton, 148, 181
Currie, Roger, 169

D-Day, 68
Davidson,Wilf, 65
Davis, Colleen, 115
Dawes, George, 158
Deacon, Ron, 65
Dear John Letters, 126-127
Decker, Bruce, 154, 156
De Forest, Lee, 11-14, 113, 181
De Jarlis, Andy, 43, 81,
Dempsey, Jack, 24, 26, 31
Dentry, Bert, 56

Derback, Ed, 87
Diefenbaker, John, 130-131, 165,
Dixon, Fred J., 19
Doern, Russ, 174
Dominion Bridge, 94-95
Drurie, Reg, 76, 90
Duncan, Chester, 139
Dunlop, Hugh, 98-99
Dunston, Ken, 176
Dutton, Ev, 167, 175

East, Neil, 163
Eaton's, 13, 14, 18, 52, 65, 68, 162, 166, 181
Ebony and White, 42
Edmondson, Bev, 102, 103
Edwards, "Brother" Jake, 163
Edwards, Vic, 102-103, 157, 167
Egler, Pastor H.H., 170-171
Elliot, Ross, 95
Elphicke, Tiny, 59
Enns, Leonard, 107
Esaw, Johnny, 133-134
d' Eschambault, Father Antoine, 79-80
Evans, Sanford, 13, 14, 113

Faris, Mal, 149
Farm Radio Forum, 116
Fessenden, Reginald Aubrey, 11
Finlay, W.J. "Billy," 33
Forman, Dave, 158

Fort Garry Hotel, 17, 21, 28-29
Fraser, Colin, 176
Freed, Alan, 145
French Heure, 78
Friesen, David K., 103, 107, 110
Friesen, "Ted", 107,
Fritzsche, Wolfgang (Buster Beau Dean), 163
Fry, Roy, 100
Funeral announcements, 98, 111
Fyfe, Peggy, 65

Gallagher, George, 97, 98
Gardner, Cliff 91, 124-126, 135, 171, 182
Garside, Les, 32, 104, 106
Garson, Stuart, 80, 83, 85, 86
Germain, Russ, 158
Gillespie, Michael, 159,
Good Deed Club, 64-65
Guess Who, 65, 148, 149, 154
Guest, Bill, 176-177,
Gunn, Bruce, 109
Guthrie, Tyrone, 29
Guyot, Dr. Henri, 80
Grant, Peter, 162-163
Greene, Monte, 74
Gregorash, Joey, 149
Griffiths, Frank, 159

Halinda, Steve, 165, 169
Hanks, Daniel "Chuck Dan," 157

Happy Gang, 63, 71, 73,
Harris, Neil, 121
Harvard, John, 102, 173, 178-179
Haslam, Jerry, 174, 178
Hemphill Trade School, 18
Henderson, Helen, 98
Henderson, Jack, 98
Hewitt, Foster, 47, 62-63, 71, 105, 134, 140, 182
Hildebrand, Elmer, 104-05, 109-111, 176, 182
Hilliard, Jim, 156-157
Hodgkinson, Brian, 65-68
Holden, Waldo, 92
Holmes, Art, 57
Holmes, Jack, 65
Hooper, Bert, 90
Hopkins, Michael, 143, 156
Horch, Ben, 105, 107
Horch, Esther, 106
Horsefield, Rev. Rae, 49-50
Howard, Hughes, 46
Huck, Barbara, 177
Hughes, Richard Digby, 100-101, 143
Hughes, Richard "Red," 102

If Day, 62
Information Radio, 174-178
Inland Broadcasting, 104, 114
Irving, Bob, 142
Irving Plum Orchestra, 29

Jackson, Les, 56
Jackson, Peter, 145
Jacobs, Jack "Indian," 140-141
Joe Pyne Show, 171
Johns, George, 150
Juba, Stephen, 165
Juneau, Pierre, 161

Kale, Jim, 154
Kannawin, John, 57
Kielback, Curt, 85
Keilback, Jim, 85
Kelvin Technical School, 14
Kennedy assassination, 131
KHJ Los Angeles, 150
King George VI, 50-53
King, Mackenzie, 38, 41, 130,
Kirton, Don, 126, 128, 142-143, 170-171
Klassen, Dorothy, 110
Knowles, Bob, 114
Knowles, Joe, 94, 95
Komar, Ted, 65,
Kozak, Boyd, 149-151
Kroeker, Harv, 110
Kroeker, Walter, 103, 105, 106, 110
Ku Klux Klan, 38

La Riviere, 157
Laurson, Marguerite, 138
Lazeruk, Basil, 98

Legge, Ron "Keg," 127, 149
Legree, George, 174
Leishman, Ken, 169
Lennon, John, 156, 173-174
Le Mesurier, Ivan (Lee Major), 174, 177, 192
Leslie Bell Singers, 92, 140
Lewis, Hedi, 158
Lill, Wendy, 177
Ljungh, Esse, 42-43
Lockerbie, Beth, 65, 92
Lowry, John E. 21-23, 28, 30-33, 39, 44, 47,
    71, 113

MacAulay, Dwight, 141
Mackenzie, Gisele, 80
MacLennan, Rory, 74-75, 162, 171, 176, 179
MacPherson, Stewart, 58-60, 165, 182
Maillard, Joe, 97
Manitoba Agricultural College, 31
Manitoba Flood Relief Fund, 91-92
Manitoba *Free Press* radio station, 16-17
Manitoba Telephone System, 21-22, 27-28, 30,
    32, 39, 44-45, 71, 82, 92
Marconi Company, 17-18, 24
Marsh, Gren, 146
McCance, Gertrude, 119-121, 182
McCloy, George, 74, 127
McDermid, Embree, 158
McGouran, Tom, 163
McIlraith, Doug, 136

McMillan, Bob, 151
McRae, Sharon, 156
McCrea, Ed, 87, 115, 165
McCreath, Ken, 169
McSweeny, Jim, 110,-111, 124, 143
Melownchuk, Andy, 146, 156
Messenger, Tony, 32
Metcalfe, William "Bill," 55-56
Micklewright, Norm, 65
Miles, Rev. Bruce, 74
Millican, Jim, 161
Milroy, Tom, 163
Moffat, Lloyd, 158
Moffat, Randy, 158
Moir, Agatha, 177
Moore, Lionel Sr., 113-118
Morgan, Chuck, 161
Morton, Brigadier R.E.A., 89
Munich, Olympics, 136-137
Murphy, John, 102
Murray, George, 92
Mutimer, Ernie, 174, 177
Mystery Lake Broadcasting, 50

Nairn, Ernie, 136
Nanton, Gus, 142
NCI, 50
Newton, Hugh, 92
New York Times, 108
Nicolson, Ken "Friar," 127, 136

Nixon, Herb, 174
Now Flower, 158

Oakes, Ron, 133
O'Brien, Charlie, 46
O'Donnel, Jake, 174
O'Leary, John, 87
Olson, Dr. Peter, 109
Osler, Edmond Boyd, 72

Parker, Murray, 136
Parr, Marc, 149
Parton, Ken, 97, 98,
Paschke, Bob, 109
Patterson, Dudley, 65, 76, 127
Pattison, Jim, 159, 161
Pattison, Mary Rogers, 115
Paulson, Jim, 150
Pearl, Bert, 43, 63, 64, 182
Penner, Ollie, 109
Pepper, Calvin, 65
Percy, Don, 163
Picken, R.J., 135-136
Pierce, John, 167
Plaunt, Allan, 39
Potoski, Dr. Michael, 97
Poyser, Alice, 177
Price, George, 118
Provost, Darrell, 159

Radio Ouest Francaise, 77-79
Rae, Jim, 116-117, 176
Ragland, Edna "Rassy," 167
Rattray, Graham, 42
Reimer, Phil, 136
Richardson, Dawson, 32, 47, 113
Richardson, James Armstrong, 31, 69
Richardson, Pehlman, 61
Roberts, Frank, 156, 167
Roberts, Herb, 21, 28-29, 30, 42, 46
Robertson, Heather, 169
Roman, Duff, 159
Rogers, Edward Samuel, "Ted," 35
Royal Alexandra Hotel, 12-14, 32
Royal Winter Fair (Brandon), 115, 118
Rutland, F.P., 33
Rural Electrification, 71

Salton, Lynn V., 15-17
Saunders, Ray, 107
Schreyer, Edward, 81, 173
Scott, Dean, 145, 157
Scott, Jack, 92
Shapira, Jack, 159
Shaw, Lillian, 86
Sifton family, 69
Slade, Don, 150, 177
Smith, Matt, 56
Songs and Music of Ukraine, 98
Sony Corporation, 129

Spry, Graham, 39,
St. Germain, Ray, 147
Steen, Anne, 154
Steen, Irving "Doc," 127, 149-150, 154
Stewart, Bill, 76, 169
Styles, Joanne, 177

Taylor, Harry, 153, 166
Television CBWT, 123-124
Television CJAY 156, 165, 167
The Beatles, 155-156
The Deverons, 148
The Jacksons, 78, 115-116
The Jury, 148
The Mongrels, 149
The Shags, 148
The Squires, 151, 153
Thiessen, A.J., 103, 106
Thornton, Henry Sir., 27, 30
Thorsteinson, Jan, 158
Todd, Gary, 145, 192
Transistor radio, 129
Trebilcoe, Bill, 167, 171-172, 174
Trudeau, Pierre, 161
Turnbull, Jack, 177, 178
Tweed, Tommy, 61, 182

Uncle Peter, 119
Unger, Walter, 136
Updike, Larry, 163

Waight, George, 62, 86
Walker, Bill, 124, 127
Warnock, "Tommy", 97-98
Warren, Peter, 165, 179-180
Waters, Allan, 146
Weir, Austin, 113
Wells, Eric, 165
Wells, Jack, 59, 126-127, 137-143, 165, 182
Westburg, Linus, 99
Whitebread, Edith, 60, 65
Whitney, Charles "Buck," 50
Whittal, Peter, 114
Wiebe, David, 110
Wire recorders, 69
Wilson, Bob, 65
Winnipeg Blue Bombers, 46, 125, 133, 140
Winnipeg Falcons, 33
Winnipeg Goldeyes, 133
Winnipeg Press Club, 165, 171
Winnipeg Tribune radio station, 17, 19-20
Winnipeg Warriors, 133
Wittman, Don, 136-137, 176, 182
Wolfman Jack, 146
Wood, Dan, 65
Wood, J. Robert, 151, 156, 182
Woods, C.M. "Dibbs", 65, 67
Woodsworth, J.S., 38

XWA, 18, 26
XWB, 14

Youngbloods of Beaver Bend, 42-23
Young, Neil, 151, 153, 167, 181
Young, Rusty, 46